MILD & BITTER WERE THE DAYS

KEN BARLOW

MILD & BITTER WERE THE DAYS

All The Best...

[signature]

KENBAR PUBLICATIONS

MILD & BITTER WERE THE DAYS
by Ken Barlow

No part of this may be reproduced or transmitted in any form
or by any other means without express permission from the authors,
unless for review purposes

First published August 2009 by Kenbar Publications
ken@mildandbitter.co.uk www.mildandbitter.co.uk
Copyright © Kenbar Publications

The moral right of the author has been asserted

Design and Artwork by Andy, andrew.greenhalgh05@btinternet.com

Printed and bound by 1010 Printing International Ltd

ISBN: 978-0-9562380-0-9

Contents

Acknowledgements

I would like to thank the following for their support, encouragement and advice throughout the compilation of this book:

Massive thanks to my wife, *Jackie,* and all my family who have tolerated, possibly welcomed my frequent and sometimes lengthy absences in researching and writing this book. Particular thanks to *Emma,* my youngest daughter who provided much need technical advice on media matters. To *Callum,* my grandson, who has been one of the inspirations for writing the book. I always wanted to leave a legacy to explain that we were all young and daft once.

To *Martin 'Jimmy' Tarbuck, Andy Vaughan, Tony Topping* and *Les Bagg.* With particular thanks to Jimmy without whose constant encouragement and immediate responses to my cries for help I would most probably have given up on the entire project.

To *Paul Benbow;* thanks for the inspiration behind the title and for being my secondary memory. Our combined memories enabled some of the more obscure diary entries to make sense, well sort of.

To *'Sir' Gordon Milne;* not only for producing one of the most thrilling football teams I have witnessed but also for taking the time to be interviewed for this book. It was an honour and a privilege to speak to Gordon. Once I got over being awe-struck, he was, as ever, a gentleman to deal with.

To *Geoff Davies;* for his interview freely given to Tony Topping some time ago but so appropriate for the times I have tried to capture within these pages.

Special thanks to *Rod Macdonald;* for his diligent and meticulous proof-reading and technical help. Any errors that remain are mine entirely. Although I have made minor amendments to the diary entries to make them readable, major grammar and punctuation errors may remain. This is because I have endeavoured to leave them largely as they were written at the time, that is to say, very poorly!

To *Andy Greenhalgh;* for the superb design and lay-out. Your flair, patience, advice, and opinions have proved utterly invaluable.

Finally; to the *people of Wigan,* Latics fans in particular. Where it appeared prudent to do so, I have tried to obscure your identity, hopefully without being over zealous about it.

Credits

The 'Wigan Observer.'

Rothman's Football Yearbook.

The 'Lancashire Evening Post & Chronicle.'

'The History Shop.' Wigan Metropolitan Council.

Wikipedia.

Harvest Records.

Kris Gray, and the Edgar Broughton Band.

By kind permission of 'The Football League.'
© The Football League Ltd.

By kind permission of 'The Northern Premier League.'
© The Northern Premier League Ltd.

'Alf Tupper, The Tough of the Track.' By kind permission of
© D.C. Thomson & Co Ltd.

My Personal Scrap Books of 1969 to 1971.

My Diary of 1970; almost in one piece.

All efforts have been made to seek permission to reproduce materials within the book. It has been a difficult process. If I have unintentionally omitted any such consent please accept my humble apologies and contact me to make matters right.

Glossary of Terms

The 'Wiggin' dialect of 1970 is much changed to today although some phrases remain in use, largely by the older generation. A classic example being… **"Nerladartgoowinonetalreet?"**

This would be spoken as a one word greeting and translates to… "now friend, how you getting on, are you well?"

Other words and phrases which may appear in the diary include:

Avgotfot	I have to.
Bint	Stupid female, girl.
Blown 'em	Mad, daft, of questionable mental health.
Bounced	Beaten up, assaulted.
Brast	Hit, fight, punch.
Chauved	Wound up, jibed, teased.
Chep	Poor, cheap, rubbish (see 'Pot').
Cottered	Hit, struck, (usually over the back of the head).
Cowd	Cold.
Far	Ugly, unpleasant to behold.
Favvas	Looks like.
Mardy	Soft or cowardly.
Klammin or Klempt	Hungry.
Looks Well	'It's a fine thing when' or ridiculous, stupid, daft.
Mard	Soft, cowardly.
Nowt	Nothing.
Pot	Poor, rubbish, disappointing.
Rare 'Un	Loss of temper, a strop or emotional outburst.
Reet	Right.
Skrikes	Cries, weeps.
Tintintin	It is not in the tin.
Wench	Girl, female, woman.
Whacked	Hit, or more commonly: playing truant from school or classes.
Wick	Terrible, rough, bad.
Wom	Home.
Yonmon	Him (over there).

Dedicated to my mum and dad.

'I gave you grief, I lied, I tried.

You gave me love personified.'

(K. R. Barlow 2003)

Introduction

Myself

It has often been said that 'youth is wasted on the young' and this diary may suggest that this maxim is not far wrong. Having just turned 16 years old I knew everything. I was opinionated, bigoted, unwittingly sexist and racist. Oh yes and truculent. My friends and I were anti-establishment, dismissive of the given order of things and knew everything. Any figure of authority was treated with utter disdain and derision. WE were the new order, WE would change the world, we just needed to get out of bed and have a beer or two first.

In short; my friends and I struggled manfully to uphold and preserve the negative stereotype of adolescents for generations to come. I think we were successful in this regard; we certainly worked hard at it. Perhaps our success was thanks to our being so well balanced with a large chip on each shoulder.

As for me personally, in 1970 what I didn't know wasn't worth knowing anyway. I was a typically obnoxious teenager; spotty, self-centred and indignant at the world at large. If a paedophile had been grooming me he would have asked for his sweeties back. It was a good job my mother loved me.

Imbued with the brio and brash certainty of youth, how did the shiny new pennies of 1970 become the tarnished old coppers of 2009? Just how did we become the 'grumpy old men and women' of our generation?

What prompted the diary keeping is a mystery to this day. I was not the diary keeping type. I could barely do my much needed homework

The author as a cheeky faced 16 year old

so why I convinced myself of the need to record my life I do not know. Perhaps it was an inflated sense of self-importance that prompted the idea? Or maybe I was influenced by 'Star Trek' and James T. Kirk's 'Captain's Log?' I was certainly obsessed about the timing of events, even down to recording specific times I left the house and returned!

UK

Back on planet earth, Britain 1970 was on the cusp of massive, industrial, social and economic change, though few realised it at the time. Both Tory and Labour governments desperately fought to retain control of major institutions, particularly on the industrial front where the all powerful trade unions were flexing their muscles with increasing militancy. Many heavy industries were facing a bleak future with little updating or investment in machinery, work practice, or marketing strategies.

Wigan

Wigan was typical of many Northern towns in 1970. Located midway between Liverpool and Manchester, the town had relied heavily on cotton and coal for employment. As these industries faded they were replaced with heavy engineering, manufacturing and, with improved transport links, distribution, as the basis for employment. These too were beginning to feel the early effects of what was to prove to be a spiralling descent into industrial meltdown.

One glimpse of the future was the Heinz factory at Kitt Green where ex-miners and engineers would count and package baked beans and some of the other 56 varieties. In short, Wigan in 1970 was a gloomy, dreary place, but to me it was home and I knew no different.

My Family

My family consisted of my parents, three brothers and an older, recently married sister, Janet aged twenty-one who had just moved out, thank God! This meant a room of my own for the first time in my life.

There was a brother three years younger than me, Robert, with whom I fought constantly, and I mean physically fought. The little sod pinched my football programmes and sold them at school, I had to pay school-pals to get my own possessions back!

Robert was fickle and contradictory by nature. He would wear T-shirts in winter and woolly jumpers in summer. He would decline the offer of a sweet then take the packet when no-one was looking! I don't think Robert ever saw the world as the rest of us did. But he was determined and independent of thought and action. Often caring and thoughtful he had the good sense to never marry and has made his own way in the world where has eventually found his niche in life as a carer for people with multi-disabilities.

Clive was six years old and the older of the two 'kids'. Dark and swarthy in complexion coupled with long eye-lashes he was positively Latin in appearance. God only knows where those genes came from! He was popular with my older sister and her friends who fussed over him as only teenage girls can. It seemed to me at the time that Clive spent the first few years of his life in the local shops and coffee bars of Wigan. Now settled on Tyneside he eventually made a career for himself in the Civil Service.

> In short, Wigan in 1970 was a gloomy, dreary place, but to me it was home and I knew no different

Mark was the tot of the family, just three years old; he was a bundle of energy as only three year-olds can be. Mark never sat still for long, he was also an inveterate dismantler of anything that could be dismantled; toy cars, trains or teddy bears. Unsurprisingly Mark now works on the production line at the Nissan car plant in Sunderland where he holds the distinction of being the only Latics supporter in the entire factory.

He and Clive constantly squabbled throughout 1970; they still do for that matter. But they both provided a much needed source of baby-sitting revenue at the time and a justification for Paul and I to play with toys we really should have had no interest in, like Action Man, blow-football and pedal-cars.

Then there was my mum and dad. Mum, Sheila, was 47 years old and a very busy mother and housewife. She also worked part-time in a local shop to boost the family finances. She was a 'softy' with a hard core; pushed to the limit she could explode!

Dad, Wilf, was 51 and worked in local government as a Rating and Valuation Officer. He was a disciplinarian of the first order, a strict authoritarian who would tolerate no back-chat. Dad's word was final. To be fair, by 1970 he had mellowed to the point of generously giving a moment's notice of a clip around the ear, just enough time to flinch.

We also had pets galore: fish, hamsters, guinea pigs, dogs cats, tortoises (pronounced 'toy-toyce' in Wigan), and even terrapins!

Compared to some we were financially well off, to others we were clearly not. We never knew poverty, but none of us ever only had to ask to get what we wanted. With seven mouths to feed everything had to be affordable by the whole. We were all encouraged to work. My sister, brother and myself all had paper-rounds; pocket money had to be earned through the week. No chores meant no pocket money. We all lived in a 3 bed-roomed detached house in a newly created housing estate. It was comfortable, 'normal' and home.

Music

On the UK music front the carefree 'hippie' influence was giving way to a more earthy, if 'glam' rock/blues music style with the emergence of Led Zeppelin, Deep Purple and T Rex whilst the pop charts were increasingly dominated by the soul sound imported from the USA to do battle with the established post-Beatle, UK pop aristocracy. This contrast of musical styles and taste was replicated in Wigan where the popular venues such as the Wigan Casino/Beachcomber, the Pink Elephant Club and Monaco played pop music heavily laced with Tamla Motown. To seek out rock/blues music it was essential to explore the underbelly of Wigan's musical scene, largely centred on the Technical College students' social scene.

Football

In football, at the beginning of 1970 Everton were the current league champions. Manchester City held the FA Cup at the start of the season with Chelsea succeeding them but it was to be Manchester United, Arsenal and the ever-improving Liverpool and Leeds United that were to dominate the decade to come in one form or another. England, at the start of the year anyway, were still World Cup holders, though this was to change later.

Wigan Athletic FC, ('Latics') the local football club, had just two years previously, left the Cheshire League to become founder members of the Northern Premier League. It was to be a year to remember for many sixteen year-old football fans growing up in the North West of England and for one Wigan fan in particular. Surrounded by established

Football League clubs, Wigan Athletic were definitely small beer in footballing terms.

There was a strange ambivalence in terms of self-esteem however – we (Latics) were giants in non-league terms but dwarves in the broader world of football. In 1970 there was no entry to the Football League through promotion, no pyramid system or Conference League. Clubs had to be voted in. There were certainly no televised non-league games and no non-league results on TV either. Our national profile was limited, to say the least.

Alf Tupper. Choice reading in 1970

Wigan Athletics' main rivals were the Cheshire county set of Macclesfield and Altrincham. We were the working class riff-raff to their public school toffs. Wigan Athletic were the Alf Tupper of northern non-league circles.

Their grounds were much smaller than ours but were well maintained, always painted spick and span. Springfield Park on the other hand was a never-ending money pit, with half-completed terracing and shabby paintwork. We just 'knew' we were better than our rivals, it was an absolute, an unchallenged belief, and to be fair, on the pitch we usually were. Stafford Rangers, Boston United, Chorley even little Skelmersdale United were bitter rivals but respected as being worthy opponents. Macclesfield and Altrincham were objects of hate, (think Liverpool and Manchester Utd or Rangers and Aberdeen). There weren't always obvious reasons why you hate them more any one else, you just did.

Personally I hated Altrincham the most. Bankrolled by wealthy businessmen, I felt a distinct inferiority complex whenever we visited their ground, Moss Lane. Perhaps it was this that led to the primeval urge to deface and spoil their pretty little home and annihilate the bastards on the pitch. In 1994 Wigan Athletic were well established as a bona fide Football League club. Losing at home to Altrincham, of all teams, in the FA Cup, utterly ruined my Christmas that year.

In 1970 even Wigan Rugby League club failed to engender the same kind of emotions as Macclesfield and Altrincham, at least the rugby lot were our home town team. I had even been to a couple of rugby league games. It just didn't 'do it' for me. Extremely large people in ill-fitting kit seemed to just rush at each other, fall over, then once this had happened a few times, either kick or give the ball to the opposition whereupon they started all over again. Even more absurd to me at the time, when a team had conceded a try, they had to kick the ball straight back to the opposition. To the local rugby league fans we were pretty much an irrelevance, a flea-on-the back-of-a-mammoth. And we were treated as such. They despised us, we despised them. It was the natural order of things in 1970 Wigan.

Occasionally some of the rugby fans would try to 'take' our terraces at Springfield Park. They were given short shrift but in truth it was a half hearted affair on both sides. It was difficult to generate the necessary blind hatred to punch someone in the face at a football match when they may well be sitting next to you at school the following day. Similarly, why kick out at someone in a terracing fracas when he was a team mate in the school football team? We were, of course, never so stupid as to visit Central Park, the rugby team's home ground mob handed, we knew our place.

Summary

This then, is the setting for the book. Based on an actual daily diary kept throughout the year of 1970 it is a wry, sometimes sardonic, look back at a year in the life of a 16 year-old lad typically perplexed by life. The author of the book is the author of the diary but separated by nearly 40 years of so called acquired wisdom and written with the benefit of hindsight. This is not a revisionist re-stating of history, nor is it an 'Adrian Molesque' or a 'Bridget Jones-ish piece of fiction. The diary is reproduced virtually verbatim but with a retrospective commentary highlighting and elaborating on the experiences recorded. At times refreshingly honest, the diary reveals many of the common core experiences of adolescence. Embarrassing to read now, yet nostalgic and bittersweet at the same time, please, dear readers, bear with the awful grammar, phonetic spelling and clumsy use of dialect, I wur only a young un!

At no time have I intended to offend. Where I felt it appropriate to do so I have protected the guilty! We have all grown up since the days this diary records but if I have caused any embarrassment to anyone, please accept my sincere apologies.

There is an old adage that states the following; Knowing that a tomato is a fruit may demonstrate knowledge but knowing not to put a tomato in a fruit salad demonstrates wisdom. This diary suggests that the acquisition of wisdom begins at an early stage and can be a painful process.

Ken Barlow

JANUARY 1970

SNOW, WIGS AND NEW MANAGEMENT...

Christmas 1969 came and went uneventfully in my life. Unlike most of the UK I had resisted the urge to buy the Christmas number one record, the thought of climbing on a wooden horse with Rolf Harris haunted my dreams.

The love of my life, Wigan Athletic Football Club (Latics), had contrived to lose all three games in December including a less than festive 1–2 defeat on Boxing Day at the mighty Great Harwood. My memories of that particular Christmas are hazy, my mental defence mechanisms having done their job efficiently.

New Year's Eve afternoon was spent, as were long periods of my life, at Springfield Park, the home of Wigan Athletic. Workmen were erecting a new loud speaker system and tea bar along the St. Andrew's Drive or 'Popular' side of the ground.

At night I saw the New-Year in at the 'Beachcomber' (better known to us local youngsters with derision as the 'Tufty Club' due to the youthful age of its customers). The Beachcomber was the basement of the later to be famous 'Wigan Casino'. It was less than salubrious, viewed variously as scruffy, run down and unkempt, or informal, relaxed and atmospheric. It did have a cloak-room, a stage, a dance floor and a refreshment bar serving pop and crisps only. To many of us it was the only place to go.

December 31st, Wednesday; 1969... "It cost me 10s to get in, thieving bastards, that's most of my Christmas money gone already. Spent most of the night chatting to Val and eventually kissed her but she wouldn't go with me because she was courting she said. So why kiss me? A bit odd that, I just don't understand wenches at all.

Came home at 1.20am. Crept in fearful of waking my parents. Had to get up at 2.30am to let Dad in."

January 1st, Thursday; 1970... "Slept in, trying to snow outside. Mooched around Wigan town centre where I met other bored girlfriends, Sue *(Sayes)*, Judith and 'Crumpets'. I really fancy Sue, she's reet fit and no danger."

Sue was referred to throughout the diary as she was known at the time, 'Sayes'. She was to have an increasingly influential effect on my life as the diary progressed, (and for some years afterward).

Sue was of medium height but well rounded in all the right places, blonde to auburn hair and always fashionably dressed. She was bright, diligent at her schoolwork and usually far too sensible for my liking! It was no surprise to any of us who knew her that Sue went on to become a doctor. Articulate, confident, outgoing, thoughtful, considerate and funny (I think that is quite enough fawning for now). Sue set the bar for my expectations of the opposite sex for years to come.

Sadly for me, at the start of 1970, Sayes was strictly out of bounds. She was my best friend's girl. Given this fact I made no play for her, nor even considered her within my reach had this not been the case. The diary goes on to demonstrate just how life can change. Two of the important lessons I learnt in 1970 were, 'never say never', and, 'you have to buy a ticket if you want to win the lottery'.

> "Went to Beachcomber again at night, asked Val out, she said no, swine. Paul reckons she is just playing hard to get and quite likes me really. That's what friends are for, lying to cheer you up. Some New Years day this has turned out to be..."

I was getting by on ten shillings a week pocket money and whatever baby-sitting money I could earn. This varied between 2s 6d and 5s 6d per evening depending on who was paying. My parents were usually the least generous whilst neighbours more so.

The local newspaper, 'The Wigan Observer' was advertising holidays abroad in Ibiza for a week costing £30 12s 0d. and a gent's suit for £10

My Spiritual Home, Springfield Park, Wigan

19s 6d. Meanwhile a ¼lb of PG Tips would set you back 1s 4d and a tin of Heinz soup 10d, and both with Green Shield stamps.

January 2nd, Friday... "Slept in all morning. Flu bug around but no one I know has it. Called for Paul and went into town for a coffee but nowt doing so we went to Latics.

They are coming on with the new tea bar. Talked to Jimmy Baker for a bit then went home. Went Beachcomber and Shirley and Val came in drunk! John finished with Shirley and she started crying. In the end Don, the door man, took her and Val home in his car. I still like Shirley a lot and I must ask her out now she and John have finished.

John asked Catherine for me but she said didn't know me at all so 'no'. Dad bought a suit today and it rained all day, is there a connection?"

January 3rd, Saturday... "Went for Paul but he was out so I went into town, nowt doing so I came home, had dinner and watched 'On The Ball'.

I'd met Marie in town and I don't think I'll go to Steve's party. Went to Latics in the afternoon, good game. We were twice behind and equalized in the last minute." *(Northern Premier League (NPL), vs Bangor City, 2–2. Scorers: Ross and Cairney. Attendance: 1,996.)*

"Went Beachcomber at night but first got drunk at Paul's on sherry, beer, martini, gin etc. Tufty club weren't bad but Shirley and Val didn't go so I went to sleep most of the time. Went in the Commercial after where John bought me a pint. I decided I would go to Steve's party after all, it were good too! Light's off and start snoggin'!"

January 4th, Sunday... "Stayed in all morning, very cold out, watched football on TV.

Went to Tufty Club at night. One of the better nights, two lads got kicked out. Bes nearly went too. A girl was after stabbin' a lass with her steel comb so Johnny Ras stopped her, all very good. Shirley and Val were there and I got talking to Shirley mostly. I bought her some cigs, with her money of course, and I've decided I'm going to ask her to go with me tomorrow. Saw Mick coming home, he says he can get us tickets for The Monaco so here we come!"

January 5th, Monday... "I find I have no paper for my Geography topic so I'll have to leave it I suppose. Danny gave me a good cord jacket today, not bad. I went to Tech in the afternoon with Paul. Very cold and snowing all evening. FA Cup draw was on at dinner-time; Man Utd vs Man City!

Went Tufty Club again at night. Pix didn't go nor Shirley or Val and it wur pot. As I am writing this I am in a bad mood and must see Shirley soon. I did see her in the shop where she works today for the first time. There's a snow storm outside as I write, thunder and lightning too, lovely."

January 6th, Tuesday... "Stayed in all morning as it was very cold out. Snow on the ground and it's frozen over. Went to Latics seething because they've sacked our manager, Ian McNeill, the fools. Then I went into Wigan to look around but nowt doing so I went in the reference library. Funny place that, all quiet and mysterious. Full of old men reading newspapers and lots of coughing going on!

I made preparations for the Arnold game; paint spray, ticker-tape, bus tickets etc, etc. Chep school tomorrow, still I'm free all morning so it can't be all bad can it? I mucked about in Wigan all evening but it was cold. Too cold to write any more."

> The Tufty Club was somewhere to go when the only other alternative was table tennis in cold church halls

Life continued in much the same vein, with nights spent at the Beachcomber and days spent suffering the apparent pointlessness of school. At the time, being a Wigan Athletic fan, even in Wigan, was to be in a distinct minority. Fading Bolton, the still entertaining Manchester United and Liverpool took most kids' loyalties in football terms, whilst Wigan Rugby dominated the town. We Latics fans banded together, making up in bravado for what we lacked in numbers.

The Tufty Club was somewhere to go when the only other alternative was table tennis in cold church halls with concave ping-pong balls where we were surrounded by well meaning parental fusspots. The last resort, often preferred, was cold street corners.

Family life was different again with three younger brothers aged 3, 6 and 13 and an older sister just moved out having married. My parents were quite strict. Dad in particular took no prisoners. We behaved or received a 'thru'penny one' often with a rolled up magazine, sometimes with the back of his hard, bony hand.

Home was solid, secure and permanent, I knew I was loved but sometimes, in the angst of adolescence, I couldn't always see this as being the case. I certainly knew I was watched over and if truth be told I needed to be, and somewhere deep down I knew it.

Night times were spent scratching around the town centre, bored and up to mischief. We spent a lot of time trying to find ways of getting money. I'd given up the 'uncool' paper round at Sharrocks' newsagents on Queensway, whilst pocket money barely paid enough to keep me in fags. The Bingo Hall looked promising with an unguarded till, but we were afraid to take the risk of finding out if there was anything in it, or the potential consequences of doing so.

January 7th, Wednesday... "First day back at school, rotten! I went with Paul to book for the Arnold cup tie away, but the booking office was closed so we walked around town and saw Val eating a cream bun that she spilt all down her herself.

Went into town at neet, met Brocky. He's as mad as a box of frogs he is. At the arcade, he showed us how he had made 9s 3d with a bit of wire off the 'Penny Falls'. A good laugh until the old cadger caught us and chased us off. Later Brocky phoned his bird and had a big row with her. Wished I had a girl to row with. Went home and watched soccer on TV."

January 8th, Thursday... "Pot school again but it's only three months to the exams! It started snowing about two hours ago and it has been a raging blizzard ever since and this is on top of four inches already down so... great!!

Booked my ticket for Arnold this afternoon, 22 shillings it cost too, never mind. "We're all off to Arnold." I whacked Geography this afternoon; Jack Sharrock saw me but said nowt."

"I stayed in this evening intending doing some homework but watched television instead. I am about to have a bath *(trumpet call!)* and must ask Shirley out tomorrow."

January 9th, Friday... "Felt lousy all day but decided to go to Tufty Club and ask Shirley to go with me. All rehearsed and finally up for it, she never turned up, she'd caught flu! If Crumpets asks me to go with her again I'll go mad. Went to bed early, feeling rough but its Arnold tomorrow!! Snow finally melted, rain and warm."

Wigan Athletic were the love of my life, still are in many respects. In the middle of boring Geography lessons with teachers like Jack Sharrock twittering on about grain yields in Canada or AVA Brown, another of our long suffering teachers, trying to teach us Tech Drawing (I'd spend the lesson drawing futuristic football stadiums), my only incentive to get through the day was 'Latics'! We could almost smell the liniment from Gidlow School. I would frequently go to the ground at lunch-time just to be there.

Away games always had a real buzz about them and an away trip, this time to Arnold FC in the new FA trophy, had a special atmosphere of glorious expectancy.

January 10th, Saturday... ♪ "With a knock kneed chicken and a bow legged hen I've never been so happy since I don't know when!!" ♪ "etc. What a day! Felt groggy going down on the coach but Jimmy and Don were always good for a laugh, with beer and butties. Crashed into the ground, just a park really, and had a riot. 4–1 up at half time and won 5–2, a Benny Cairney hat-trick. Wembley, Wembley here we come! Poured down all day but I felt OK. We nearly got bounced at a motorway cafe by a group of Stoke City fans but just got away with it."

January 11th, Sunday... "Stayed in all day but for the evening. Read the Sunday papers, not much in about Latics and the 'Sunday Express' said Arnold 2–2 Wigan! Shocking eh?

I contemplated doing my English homework but I'm not sure which I am supposed to do. I felt a lot better today; only thing is a bad cough and sore throat."

"I watched Man Utd beat Arsenal 2–1 on TV." *(Football League Div One. Scorers: Willie Morgan and Carlo Sartori. Att: 41,055.)*

"Went to Beachcomber at night but neither Val nor Shirley came, probably still got flu. Some rotten girl asked me but Ugh, no thanks. FA trophy draw tomorrow, here's hoping for an easy home draw."

January 12th, Monday... "I hate Mondays at school. I whacked Jack's again and I hid in a cupboard when he came into room four! I paid my library fine today too.

I went to Latics at dinner-time to find out who we had drawn in the FA trophy. Telford away, managed by Ron Flowers too. Still it could have been worse. Went to the Beachcomber but it was rotten, worse than that it was 'sh...you know what'. Val came later and I saw her after when she was with that Stey lad but I didn't talk to her proper. We saw some Liverpool fans coming off the train-station; they won 3–0, lucky dogs."

January 13th, Tuesday... "I think this is the worst day on my timetable. Double Maths with Korky. It's bloody rotten, dead boring, all about hypotenuse, sines and cosines... rubbish. Then it's double art after dinner. I've started on an oil painting and it is coming along, slowly. Then we have double English again, Harry Holland made us do all our corrections all lesson, so boring. Actually I felt like fainting in assembly this morning and had to leave, but I feel alright again now.

I stayed in at night, watched TV and cut my own hair. Ugh."

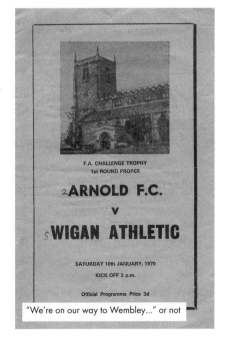

F.A. CHALLENGE TROPHY
1st ROUND PROPER

2 **ARNOLD F.C.**

v

5 **WIGAN ATHLETIC**

SATURDAY 10th JANUARY, 1970
KICK OFF 3 p.m.

Official Programme Price 3d

"We're on our way to Wembley..." or not

Going to the barbers was deemed to be an unnecessary expense. We would cut our own hair even though the results were often hilarious. (We riff-raff wouldn't use 'poncy hairdressers' in those days, barbers at a push, maybe.) This cost-cutting exercise gradually became less commonplace as girlfriends and thus self-image came more to the fore.

January 14th, Wednesday... "It was pouring down all day and but for the fact that I had easy lessons I'm sure I would have cried. I carried on with that oil painting till break and tried to do my maths after break but without success. Mr Critchley came in and told us all about the school five-a-side competition. We did graphs with Korky, then five-a-side in the gym.

At night me and Paul went into town and wrote 'Latics' everywhere in felt tip pen! Bingo hall was a failure again. Watched England on telly, they're rotten, rotten rotten, rotten." *(vs Holland at Wembley, 0-0. Part of the pre-Mexico World Cup build up.)*

January 15th, Thursday... "Well I went to school feeling sick of it and I left feeling the same way. It's boring, childish, wasting time and pointless. There was only me who had done my English composition so we marked that and passed away the rest of the lesson doing I don't know what. In Maths we carried on with those rotten graphs again, ugh... I went in to Biology but whacked Ted's Physics lesson, he found out but never said owt.

The afternoon went quick and I actually went into Jack's Geography lesson, not sure if he recognised me! In Art I tried to carry on with my oil painting but he had no white paint.

I had to stay in and baby sit at night while Mum and Dad went out to a Dinner-Dance. Paul came round and we watched TV all night. It's very mild outside, touch wood."

January 16th, Friday... "Well I suppose there isn't long left, thank God, of school that is. I've just got no enthusiasm for it at all. School was a shambles, we all whacked classes, got caught, then piled out of the window again. Keith and I went home wondering what'll happen?"

> "I went to the Tufty Club again at night and at
> long last Shirley came. She was wearing a wig!!
> A bit strange but it's nice. I felt sick all night otherwise
> I would have asked her out. I might have a job too,
> got to phone up soon."

The news that Colonel Ghadaffi had taken control of Libya on this day in 1970 passed me by. On the other hand I don't suppose the Colonel was aware that, on that very same day, the girl I lusted after went to the Tufty Club wearing a wig. This was clearly a case of mutual and blissful ignorance between the Colonel and me. Shirley never did let it be known just why she felt the urge to wear a wig. We presumed it was just one of those zany fashion things that girls did then, as now.

Whilst the Tufty Club played Tamla Motown music almost exclusively, my musical tastes couldn't have been further removed. Blood, Sweat and Tears, John Mayall, Taste, Jethro Tull, and the new boys on the block Led Zeppelin, were all much more to my suiting. Led Zeppelin were once famously and mistakenly renamed by the headmaster at Wigan Grammar School as 'Fred' Zeppelin, midst hoots of derision, his search for 'street cred' was sunk beyond redemption.

I did not enjoy my last year at school one bit. It all seemed so irrelevant. Have I mentioned this in the introduction? I thought I might have.

> **January 17th, Saturday...** "Went into town with Paul
> this morning and I bought the new Jethro Tull single
> 'Witches' Promise' – Cost me 4/3d too, from Hurst's.
> Went Latics in the afternoon, we won 2–0 should have
> been 6 like usual. Only 1,400 on, shocking eh?" *(vs Prescot*
> *Cables in the Lancashire FA Cup. Scorers: Cairney and Gillibrand.)*
> "Went to Tufty Club at night, Shirley left soon after
> I came, no wig tonight. Paul and I got thrown out
> accused of writing 'Latics Boot Boys' all over the gents."

(Our sense of indignation and injustice at this outrage were in no way diminished by the fact that we were entirely guilty as charged.)

> **January 18th, Sunday...** "Slept in until 12 o'clock and read
> the papers. I went round to Paul's in the afternoon with
> 'Witch's Promise' and a sampler LP called 'Nice Enough To
> Eat'. We played them for a bit then watched soccer on TV."

'Nice Enough To Eat' cost me 15s 6d and was packed with real talent. Nick Drake, Traffic, Blodwyn Pig, Spooky Tooth and King Crimson to name but a few. It remains a highly prized part of my vinyl collection, scratches included.

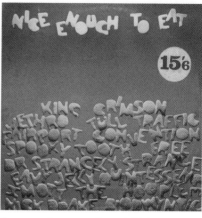

"We talked about our holidays and decided on the Isle of Wight. We'll have to wait for Paul's dad to get us on a coach before we know when it'll be.

Went to Tufty Club again at night. Shirley was supposed to go with Stey but didn't 'cos he went with someone else. I saw Val going past our house today, she doesn't usually."

School

Gidlow Boys' Secondary Modern School was definitely secondary but certainly not modern. Leaky roofs, crowded classrooms, a gym that served as a dining room, no lockers, no showers and teachers who taught by rote; repeating the same lesson as the previous 30 years or more. Well intentioned as the teachers may have been, and some of them did have their hearts in the right place, most of them suffered from chronic institutionalisation and boredom that rapidly transferred itself to the pupils.

We were deemed to be factory fodder for industries that were closing down. Myself, and many others, may have succeeded relatively in life, despite, rather than because of, our education. I now firmly believe that adult education is the key to success for many and should be recognised as such with increased government investment and political enthusiasm.

The fifth and final year at school was a tedious experience to be endured not enjoyed. The diary is littered with examples of my contempt for the whole experience.

January 19th, Monday... "I was a bit apprehensive about school after Friday's rumpus but nowt has happened yet. It wasn't a bad day at school actually. I changed my library books and finished an English Literature reader book."

"At home my dad phoned a chap about a job for me, he said he'd phone back but didn't so, try again eh dad? Latics' accounts reveal that their wage bill has risen from £6,000 p.a. to £24,000 p.a. in the 68/69 season, a bit daft that.

Paul and I have decided to go Bournemouth for our holidays. We reckon it will cost about £14 for the week. Went Tufty Club at night and I suppose I could have gone with Shirley if I'd wanted to. I'm not really that bothered now; I've been that long trying. Anyway, I'm sure she was only interested in me 'cos no-one else was around."

January 20th, Tuesday... "Worst day of the week, as I've said before, but the morning passed alright. Maths went slowly but surely. We smashed a window in Room four at dinner-time. I also bought a Latics pocket diary off Moggy for 1s 6d. I don't know why, I don't really want it, 'cos he's a mate I suppose. I've finished my oil painting in Art but I'm not sure, it still looks chep to me.

It said on the 1.30pm news that Tommy Doc will be Latics' new manager! We picked our five-a-side teams at break and I've not got a bad team I suppose.

Me and Paul went into Wigan at night but nowt doing so we went to St Michael's Church Hall where I nicked a bottle of pop. I've borrowed Jethro Tull's 'Stand Up' off Paul tonight too, it is great."

January 21st, Wednesday... "I finished my abstract face in Art today but it needs a background. I paid Mog for the diary too, now I'm skint. Double Maths was chep; we did some more algebraic graphs, rotten. We had a laugh throughout it though, putting a dirty picture on Korky's desk, throwing a smelly old pump at each other etc."

'Korky' was Mr Harold Price, the headmaster of the school. He was nick-named Korky because he reputedly had a wooden leg as a result of a war injury. Looking back he was far-sighted, long-suffering and generally of a kind disposition. He used his powers to inflict corporal punishment rarely and obviously with reluctance. I am aware that certain other pupils of my era and before may not concur with this character assessment!

"I think I've got my final five-a-side player but he may be picked. We had basketball in the gym, house matches. Raleigh lost to Nelson 24–20 and we, Gordon, beat Scott 48–4! Went to Latics ground at dinner-time, it's coming along too.

I stayed in at night. While I was writing to firms for a job and playing Jethro at the same time, a girl came to the door selling pictures. She was an art student, the pictures were great, so was she! My mum and dad bought a picture off her. I asked her if she would do my Art homework but dad told me to "get on." I watched a daft play on telly and some Lonnie Donegan show and went to bed dreaming of art students at Wigan Tech."

January 22nd, Thursday... "It was a chep day today but no matter, the time is coming for a change! I must get a job. The morning passed alright I got cottered in Pop's for answering back but it was a laugh. The same goes for the afternoon with nothing much happening, dead boring. Critchley says us fifth years can form our own football team if we want but we can't agree when to play.

Latics still have no manager, latest applicant is Roy Vernon for £3,000!

Went into town at night Paul and I, but nowt doing. Bingo till was a failure again. Jethro Tull and Chicago were both on Top of the Pops, great. Oh yes, I forgot, we set a fire extinguisher off in the bogs at school today, no-one found out so we must do it again."

January 23rd, Friday... "I am beginning to realise that the exam papers are quite hard and I will need to work hard on them if I have any chance at all. I finished off my abstract face picture in Art today so I think I'll try another oil painting next. We went through the Physics paper and it's reasonably easy but I haven't a clue in the Biology questions.

Paul and I went to Tufty Club at night. Shirley is going with Mick Trotzsko so f**k her. Nothing doing really, like usual, but it's a way to spend an evening I suppose. I feel a bit sick now that Shirley's going with Trotzsko but I had my chance didn't I?"

January 24th, Saturday... "Life goes on, and on, and on, and on... I got up mid-morning and went into town with Paul. We met Keith who was meeting up with Gerald.

Paul said he'd come round in the afternoon but never did, I didn't expect him to, he's like that sometimes. I watched rugby on the telly and occasionally turned on the radio for the Utd vs City score.

Latics lost away at Bangor 1–2 *(NPL)*. We finally scored a penalty from Mandy Hill. The report suggested that we played pretty good too. We are missing Tony McLoughlin summat rotten. United beat City 3–0." *(FA Cup 4th round, Old Trafford. Scorers: Brian Kidd x 2 and Willie Morgan.)*

"Pouring with rain, got soaked going to the Tufty Club, great group on called 'Sugar', superb they were, great change from Soul crap all night long. No sign of Shirley or Val. Susan Warren is nice, but is she really interested in me, or Paul and just being nice to me 'cos I'm his mate?"

One of the few benefits to emerge from being brainwashed with soul music was that the lyrics were easily changed to suit the terraces and the 'hook' was easy to remember. In this way the Martha Reeves song 'Jimmy Mack, when are you coming back' was readily adapted by us Latics fans to 'Tony, Tony, Oh Tony Mac, when are you coming back?' We desperately needed him too. Tony McLoughlin, our big, strong, tough centre forward, and my hero, had been suspended for three months merely for playing in a Sunday amateur league game. We all felt it very harsh and wondered if there wasn't something else that was never revealed to the public.

January 25th, Sunday... "This must rank as one of the worst weekends on record. First of all I find that Trotzsko's going with Shirley proper, then Latics lose, although Man Utd won I suppose. It was pot at Beachcomber Friday and Saturday and then I have to stay in on Sunday for economical reasons. Great isn't it?

My sister Janet and her husband Wayne came for the day with little Anthony. Still no sign of the donkey jacket

Wayne promised me. The only good thing about today was Man Utd beating Man City 3–0 on telly; they played really well for once. I just stayed in and watched telly all day, it wur chep, chep, chep. I am in a rotten mood so get lost and let me get to sleep and leave this rubbish behind me."

January 26th, Monday... "I've said before in these records that I hate Mondays and I will continue saying so until I can sleep in till 11am every Monday. I suppose it wasn't too bad really.

> First of all we broke a window in AVA's classroom! Then we set free a watch he had confiscated ages ago

The FA Cup draw was made at dinner-time and it's Tranmere or Northampton vs Man Utd so perhaps some giant killing but I hope not? Latics are probably having Gordon Milne as the new manager. Fools, where has he ever managed? Still owt's better than nowt I suppose.

Amongst other clothes I've been given by my cousin Alan Abrehart in London is a right smart sports jacket. Went Tufty Club again and guess what? It was pot again. Trotzsko finished with Shirley but she left before I could ask her. Man Utd drew with Leeds 2–2." *(1st Division. Scorers: Kidd and Sadler.)*

January 27th, Tuesday... "I have come to the conclusion that but for Maths I could have done well in my exams but, there it is. We did magazine articles in English and then it was rubbish Maths again. Art wasn't bad and we were let out at 3.15pm because the teachers had a meeting.

Latics new manager is Gordon Milne. I only hope he is a good 'un, he'll need to be or they'll sack him knowing Latics board!

At tea-time my mum told me I had to stop in all night while they went to a dinner-dance or something. Anyway I did some Art, History and English homework while playing Jethro Tull's records.

I must get some money for Telford and quick. Goodbye, sleep well."

January 28th, Wednesday... "I love Wednesdays 'cos I'm free all morning. I didn't do much because there isn't much I can do actually. At dinner time I went down to Latics, Gordon Milne was there too looking around. The ground improvements are coming along slowly but surely.

Maths was chep and AVA gave us lines to do but he knows what he can do! We, Gordon, beat Nelson 18-14 at basketball, unbeaten so far. My mum gave me 4s for baby-sitting last night so I've now got 6s.6d saved up to get to Telford.

At night Paul and I mucked about in Wigan then went home to watch soccer on TV."

January 29th, Thursday... "School is just so chep, AVA never did ask us for the lines he set us so he can fuuuuuugetem. We looked at wood under a microscope in Pop's. In Ted's we went over an old exam paper, it passes the time I suppose. I whacked Geography 'cos it's so rotten, just Jack going blah-blah-blah all day. Korky had us in his study this afternoon, just going through old exam papers, rubbish as I've said before.

I think I've got my money for the Telford away game, baby-sitting money mainly. Looking forward to Wed 4th Feb, Latics vs Darwen, Tony's back!!! Me and Paul went down to Latics and watched Gordon Milne, Tony and all the players training. Came home and had a bath."

January 30th, Friday... "Just another day after the one before it. Life is so boring sometimes isn't it? The morning went alright I suppose and so did the afternoon but it was at dinner-time that things started to happen. First of all we broke a window in AVA's classroom! Then we set free a watch he had confiscated ages ago. Finally we went to the library and were asked to leave so we shouted 'Fascist Pigs!' as we left.

I had a shave last night and it does cut down the number of spots I get. I booked to go to Telford this afternoon with Paul and Schos. Went to Beachcomber at night but Shirley didn't go and it wur pot yet again. I'm sick of saying that!"

January 31st, Saturday... "Never mind it was good for a laugh! Telford away in the FA trophy... Woke up early, went to Moggy's to borrow his 'bovver' boots but he wasn't up and his mum wouldn't lend them. Made my butties and went for Paul.

We all piled on the coach at the Gas Board showrooms at 9.15am. There was Schos, Paul, Jimmy, Don and a load of daft 'uns. We all had a good laugh on the way down. The game was chep, we hammered them, made loads of chances yet lost 0-1, dead unlucky really. Ron Flower's lot were lucky buggers and no danger! Benny Cairney was pot. No fighting, no-one to fight with, crap ground too. So, no Wembley for us this season.

Got back to Wigan about 7.45pm went to Tufty Club, nowt doing, I'm sick of that place. Still, Man United beat Derby County 1–0, Bobby Charlton scored."

So January 1970 went out with a whimper, a bit like Latics' FA trophy campaign really. School was 'pot', love life 'chep' and your diarist was not a happy chappy.

Would February bring an upturn in my life?

Could I finally find someone desperate enough to become my girlfriend?

Will the return of Tony Mac bring about a change of fortune for new manager, Gordon Milne?

FEBRUARY 1970

School, boredom, courtship behaviour and the return of a hero...

> **February 1st, Sunday...** "Well there isn't much to write
> about really. I slept in all morning, read the papers but
> 'cos Latics lost there isn't much to read about is there?
> I went round to Paul's in the afternoon and watched
> footy highlights followed by 'Please Sir' on telly.
>   There was, and still is, a biting wind outside, yet the
> weather is reasonably mild. I had a shave; I must get rid
> of these spots. Went to Tufty Club yet again, chep it wur
> too. I was going to ask Shirley but just can't. I don't know
> why, I just can't do it. Now if I was drunk well that would
> be different wouldn't it? Sleep tight Neth."

'Neth' was what my two baby brothers called myself. The lazy little
beggars could not be bothered with the 'Ken' bit. Surprisingly, given
this ineptitude at mastering language skills, they both eventually
mastered two languages... 'Geordie' and 'bad'.

> **February 2nd, Monday...** "The whole family overslept
> but I still wasn't late for school. I'm dying for school to
> end, it just gets worse each week, just pot it is. I actually
> went into Jack's Geography lesson again today.
>   Great fight at dinner-time, Rob *(Ben Grimm)* dropped
> Tommy G, his eye was all swelled up and cacka!
>   Guess where me and Paul went at night by way of
> a change? We went to the Beachcomber and it was
> rubbish, chep, neither Shirley nor Val went. I talked to
> Bes most of the night. Paul says I've to make out a list
> of girls I like for homework! Some hope he's got."

Paul and I were almost inseparable at the time. We had met five years
previously as little 11 year-olds and had started at secondary school
together. In 1970 he was of medium build with long, dark hair parted
down the middle, as was fashionable at the time. Paul was one of those
people who were somehow trendy and chic without really trying.
Furthermore he could grow a 'proper' beard, with real stubble; indeed
he often had to shave twice a day! I, on the other hand, shaved twice
a week. Whatever the 'it' factor was in 1970, Paul had it and consequently he was popular with the girls.
     We had a lot in common, Latics, music and a shared enthusiasm for

drinking alcohol being just three of the factors that bound us together. He was polite but friendly and was possessed of a great sense of 'Pythonesque' type humour. Yet at the same time he could be intense and introspective. I suppose we faced the adversities of adolescence together, leaning on each other when necessary and going our own ways at times too.

I am pleased to say that today Paul is happily married with three fabulous daughters. He remains Latics daft, still lives in Wigan and has acted as a much needed 'secondary memory' for me in clarifying some of my memories and illegible diary entries.

February 3rd, Tuesday... "I've just worked out that I have been alive for 5,920 days exactly. What a waste of time, I wish you could plan it before you live it."

Such self indulgent, existential angst, and at a time when I am fairly certain Gidlow Boys' Secondary Modern school never taught philosophy!

"I have been made editor of the school magazine and it's pot. I have to read and rewrite every article submitted. Sometimes I have to make one article out of two different ones. I did this all morning, boring. And then Maths, it was rotten too.

Jack Meredith, aka 'Popeye' *(school janitor),* snatched Grog at lunch-time. Secretly I wasn't surprised, best not try me though, janitor or not. No Art today 'cos Trencher is away so we did yet more school magazine articles till 4 o'clock.

I went to Latics at night but Paul stayed in. I watched Gordon Milne training the youth team. Oggy is a good un but he brags too much. Had a bath and went to bed, Tony Mac is back tomorrow!!"

February 4th, Wednesday... "It was pouring down in the morning so I wore a hat to school. Then it raged a blizzard, the snow was an inch thick in half an hour but then suddenly stopped. I had to take young Sorby to the nurse's clinic 'cos his ear was bleeding. The snow was melted by torrential rain and I got soaked. Evvy set fire to a desk and Korky went bald at us all."

We couldn't understand his reaction, why all the fuss? It was only arson in a school for God's sake! This was seen as a typical over-reaction from an overbearing authority figure, stifling our individuality, another brick in the wall and all that.

> "It sleeted, snowed and rained all day only drying up about 5 o'clock. I thought Latics match would be called off but thankfully not. Fantastic, we beat Darwen 11–1 with 'King' Tony McLoughlin scoring seven of 'em, great he was, never put a foot wrong. I think this is our biggest win for ages and a Latics record for Tony. *(It was.)* If only he'd played at Telford. Not many on to witness it, attendance of just 742." *(Lancashire FA Trophy. Other scorers: Fleming x 2, Fielding and Hill, pen.)*

'My Hero'; Tony McLoughlin,1970

In 1970 Wigan Athletic were of little interest to national journalists. Finding the match result was a triumph, any report of the game, a real bonus. Even the local media gave precious little coverage to their senior football team, preferring the rugby league and union teams instead. What did emerge in the local press, as a result of Tony Mac's exploits that week, was that he put his remarkable feat down to water polo training which kept him fit through his lengthy lay off. Certainly the conditions that night were ideal!

> **February 5th, Thursday...** "Woke up feeling great 'cos Latics had won 11–1 and Tony got seven. Not even a mention in the Express, but the Mirror had a good report so I bought a copy from Grundy's paper shop and cut it out for my Latics scrapbook.
> School was chep, Jack Meredith is a nosey, interfering b****** and Jack Sharrock wants us to patrol the corridors at dinner-times, some hope he's got! I traipsed

home at lunch-time for my five-a-side kit only to discover later that it was cancelled.

Paul is staying in tonight studying for his exams, swot. I worked on my art abstract picture. Spots are getting worse, despite shaving regular."

February 6th, Friday... "It was chep at school today but most of 4T have had their heads shaved into 'skinheads'! They look well!

We went to Tufty Club at night but it wur pot. My mate Pip went after Sandra Kelly but she wouldn't go with him 'cos she went with Slonks instead!

The weather has gone cold again and, as I write it is snowing heavy. I hope it stops soon, Latics are playing tomorrow and Tony wants another seven goals! I think I'll do a bit more of my abstract face for Art then read my book before bed."

February 7th, Saturday... "It was pouring down all morning and when I went round to Paul's it really started, it lashed down like a monsoon! We both thought Latics game would be called off but no, we played. Latics only drew 0-0 at home to Matlock but it wasn't a bad result really. Man Utd thrashed Northampton 8–2 away in the FA Cup with George Best scoring six!"

At the time I recall we all felt certain that George Best was inspired by Tony McLoughlin's record breaking feat a few days before.

"We went to Tufty Club at night, it wur pot again. Sayes is in a funny mood and I don't know why?"

February 8th, Sunday... "Do you know I haven't put a foot out of doors today? I woke up at 10am. God knows why, I usually have a lie-in on Sundays. Our Robert says I have stolen 2s but I haven't. Read the papers but not much in except all about United winning 8–2.

I finished off my mosaic pattern. It looks good from a few feet away. Hope the Art examiners stand a few feet away too!

Gran came for tea and gave us all some chocolate, she

is a secret Man Utd fan so we all watched the highlights on TV, they were great, so was George Best. I had to stay in and baby-sit at night so I just watched a film called 'Mrs Miniver', not bad actually."

February 9th, Monday... "Today is just one day like any other really. I whacked Geography again. Jack has told me that if I don't turn up for Geography more often he will scrub my name off the exam candidate's list. Wouldn't bother me but my dad's reaction would. I had to carry my art folder home, it was very windy with hailstones, never mind, it survived. Mum says she likes the oil paining, she must be daft!

Me and Paul went to Beachcomber at night. It was chep except at the end when I went with Shirley at last. She is a nice girl really; I don't care what others say about her."

'Going' with someone did not perhaps have quite the same connotation then as it does now. Leaving the Beachcomber, or any dance venue, with a member of the opposite sex at the end of the night was one of the ways of establishing credibility with your peers and was thus very important. In truth it invariably meant a walk to the bus stop with a brief sojourn in a shop doorway or up the side of Wigan church. If you were lucky a quick snog and a fumble would ensue, the latter usually rebuffed. It was fortunate in my case that I was used to walking home alone.

Going with someone 'proper' suggested a degree of permanence to the relationship, perhaps as long as a fortnight sometimes. Monday the 9th was clearly a red letter day for me, 'going' with Shirley obviously worth noting in the diary.

February 10th, Tuesday... "Someone has tried to say that we pinched a watch out of AVA's but we haven't really, we just returned it to its rightful owner. AVA says he has been to a solicitor. We will try to find out who telt on us and do him! AVA had us in his room at 4 o'clock telling us the legal position.

It snowed again last night and it's very cold out. I have now started a water colour in Art and it's coming out alright I suppose. In a week of records, I managed to eat a personal best of six pancakes for tea."

"Paul and I went for a scooter off Bes, it wouldn't start and we had to push it home. A copper saw us and tried to nab us but we hid in the backs and watched him go by."

February 11th, Wednesday... "I woke up in a good mood 'cos United won 1–0 at Ipswich *(Brian Kidd scorer)* and I had all morning off. It's dead cold out just now.

The morning went all right. I went down to Latics. The ground improvements are coming along good. School was its usual boring self. Critchley keeps saying we know something about the stolen watch. Maths was chep, we did graphs again and in games we played basketball between ourselves.

According to the 'Daily Mirror' Latics may play in Russia this summer, I won't be going to that away game! I watched a TV programme about George Best followed by Leicester City 0-2 Liverpool, undeserved victory. Stew Fenton rang and says the scooter will work, great!"

February 12th, Thursday... "It is bitter out at the moment so we didn't play Shevington High School. It's been rearranged for after the holidays. School is so boring, I don't notice the time passing. I can't wait to start work!

> According to the 'Daily Mirror' Latics may play in Russia this summer, I won't be going to that away game!

It is raging a blizzard everywhere in Britain according to the news on telly but for some unknown reason not in Wigan. There was a slight snow fall but only very slight. Juicy Lucy, Canned Heat and Jethro Tull were all on 'Top of the Pops', not bad. Paul and I went into town at night but it is very cold indeed so we came home early. Even the RAF greatcoat I've borrowed off Paul doesn't keep me warm in that weather.

I'm dying for a shit but Dad is in the bathroom!"

February 13th, Friday... "School was alright I suppose. Ted Ward's class was boring and Pop felt ill and went home so school wasn't bad at all today.Gordon Milne was on the back of the 'Daily Mirror' today and it looks like Latics will play in Russia in the summer!"

"Beachcomber was chep again, Shirley never showed. On the way home I found a black cat and just look at the date! It is bitterly cold and the cat is sleeping on my bed."

February 14th, Saturday... "St Valentine's day, huh, some hope!

Paul and I went into town. It was very cold. I bought some Kit-E-Kat for my kitten. I stayed in this afternoon 'cos Latics were away at Scarborough and I have no money to go." *(NPL, drew 1–1. Scorer: Iain Gillibrand. Att: 1,911. Raging blizzard, Gordon Milne's playing debut.)*

"The reserves game was postponed 'cos of the weather so I had to stay in and watched England rugby union on telly, we beat Scotland 9–3, dead boring too. Man United drew 1–1 at home with Crystal Palace. Brian Kidd scored again.

We went to Tufty Club again but it wur pot. Shirley came but I'm not being a 'take it or leave it' for her or anybody. 'Disco 2' on telly was good, 'Rock & Roll', great. I am sleeping with the cat again!"

St. Valentine's Day may as well never have happened for me. I neither sent nor received any cards. In truth I cut a lonely, lovelorn figure with only a stray cat for close company.

February 15th, Sunday... "My parents put their foot down this morning and told me that if I wanted breakfast I should get up earlier than 11.30am."

What my parents failed to realize, because it wasn't understood at the time, was that adolescents do actually need all that extra sleep. It is now accepted by neuropsychologists that extra sleep is linked to crucial brain development during adolescence. All of which means that I can safely blame my parents for my own arrested development. I have to admit however that this research was something I also conveniently overlooked when my own little darlings spent all morning deep in the arms of Morpheus when they too were teenagers.

"It seems that my new cat belongs to the new neighbours, it had run away and they want him back. I went to Paul's in the afternoon, we just talked and mucked about really, it wur chep. I stayed in at night, at 3s 6d it's too dear at the Beachcomber and too chep. Danny told me that Jim Fleming, who works for him now, was a Scottish under-23 international but got an injury. It's been snowing again tonight but not much. God Bless."

February 16th, Monday... "My hot water bottle burst last night, so I had to sleep in my sleeping bag, very warm too. Off school all week!

Clive went to the dentist in the morning so I stayed in and watched our Mark. In the afternoon I went into town and saw some pretty good shoes in Woolworth's but Dad wants to see them first.

We went to Tufty Club at night, it was chep again. There was really only Paul that I knew well. Val went and spent a lot of time with me, I wanted Paul to ask her for me but I just didn't tell him, I don't know why, I'm thick maybe that's why? Val said Shirley didn't want to come out tonight. I went home sick 'cos I never asked Val, then I watched Jekyll and Hyde on TV."

My miserable life continued. Latics were playing crap, my new found feline friend had been taken from me, I couldn't get a girlfriend and last night my hot-water bottle burst in bed, honest!

Those who know me now may be surprised to learn that I have not always been blessed with the looks of George Clooney (the cover photos do not do me justice) and, like most of the local young bucks, I lacked the confidence to ask a girl out, face to face. It was common practice to get a friend to undertake this task for you. I became increasingly adept in this role, indeed I became quite the 'go-between'. I was painfully aware that I was confident and able in this role for others but utterly incompetent at achieving the same aim for myself.

It wasn't only the boys who were shy in this respect. Girls would very rarely ask you out personally but would quite happily ask a friend to do so on their behalf. This could lead to unintentional, and sometimes planned, confusion. On occasions I was told, "My mate fancies you, will you go with her?" This would be accompanied by a vague wave in the general direction of a gaggle of giggling girls. If the girl pointed out appealed to me, the reply would be in the affirmative. However sometimes the girl that appeared at the end of the night was certainly NOT the one pointed out! Usually I was too much of a gentleman to object but the walk home would be quick and painless avoiding any shop doorways.

February 17th, Tuesday... "It snowed dead hard last night and we're all drifted up! Snow got in through Robert's bedroom window and the utility room. I couldn't open my window. I stayed at home all morning playing with my little brothers in the snow. It was so deep it nearly covered our Mark in places. He loved it. In the afternoon I went into town and went the library. I met Sayes and 'Crumpets'. The snow was all sloppy and very cold.

At night me and Paul eventually slushed our way into town, nowt doing, is there ever? Later the snow froze over so our feet weren't so wet and cold on the way home. As I write it has started snowing again. We'll be cut off tomorrow!"

February 18th, Wednesday... "When I awoke all the snow had started to melt. Off school this week, half term hols. I stayed in all morning. In the afternoon I went down to Latics, the pitch was like a huge lake! I've never seen a sight like it, one large paddy field. The worst condition I've ever seen a professional pitch in.

I stayed in at night. I must start my geography project, deadline is getting very close. TV broke down, I sat playing records so Dad put the radio on even louder, yukkk, I went for a bath. I've discovered that our Robert has nicked a library book."

Thursday, 19th February... "I posted a letter to a 'Careers Guide' in the 'Daily Express' this morning. Went into town and bought a pair of desert-wellies. They are a bit big but it was the only size they had and at 25s – well worth it. Poured down all day, went round to Paul's, played records and talked. I'm still knackered so I went to watch Latics training, Tony Mac was dead lazy and Jim Fleming dead slow! Poured down all evening and I got soaked."

These past three entries in the diary demonstrate just how mundane life was. That I went to the trouble of recording such trivia suggests that these were not the highlights of my life in 1970 but were my life. Wigan

Athletic, school and the Beachcomber remained constants, but none were exactly reason to celebrate a youthful, carefree existence.

> **February 20th, Friday...** "I copied down some wonderfully descriptive paragraphs from a book I am reading, 'Dracula'. Dead good they are. I've copied them into my English book. I'm tempted to use them in my next composition but will Harry Holland notice that it's much better than my usual work? Probably, best not.
>
> In the afternoon I changed my library books then went home for a bath. Met with Paul who showed me some plans in the paper for Latics to build a new stand for the Shevington End, superb!
>
> Went to Tufty Club at night but neither Shirley nor Val went, they go to the Rugby Club I think. We just mucked about, Bes and I and found a packet of fags with 15 still in it. Saw Paul after he had seen Sue home and we walked up with Bes. I want to go with Shirley, Val or anyone!"

Any golfers who know the Wigan area well may be interested to know that it was this week in 1970 that work started on what was eventually to become Haigh Golf Course, now a well established and very popular venue for anyone who likes to ruin a good walk.

> **February 21st, Saturday...** "Latics finally won!! First league win for 15 weeks, 2–1 away at Stafford, they're third in the league too *(NPL)*. Jim Fleming and Davy Breen scored, fantastic win. I didn't go, went to watch the reserves get beat 1–2 instead. We went into the Supporters' Club afterwards and watched the results come in on the telly. United drew 1–1 so we'll kill 'em at Old Trafford!" *(Middlesbrough, away, FA Cup. Scorer: Carlo Sartori.)*
>
> "Went to Tufty Club to celebrate, no one interested, most are rugby fans. Chep night, wish I had money to go somewhere else I'd go to all sorts of places 'cept the Beachcomber."

> **February 22nd, Sunday...** "It's chep on Sundays, always is. Not much about Latics in the papers and they said United were lucky. I cleaned my soccer boots 'cos it's Shevvy tomorrow!"

"Went round to Paul's and watched Boro 1–1 United. I suppose United were a bit lucky but Boro only have themselves to blame. Chelsea beat QPR 4–2, it was on TV too. Chelsea look a good team.

I asked Paul to come to Tufty Club at night even if I paid him in but he had too much homework, he had to read 'The History of Mr Polly'. I went by myself and I was going to ask Shirley or Val but really, they're only girls after all, so why all the fuss?"

> It was this week in 1970 that work started on what was eventually to become Haigh Golf Course

February 23rd, Monday... "I'm sick of school; it's the same week in and week out. I was free until 3pm and then it should have been History but because we were playing Shevington High we didn't go in. Everyone but Benny, Harry and I got the bus but we got a lift from Critchley in his van.

Oh! the shame of it all, we finally get to play Shevvy school after numerous postponements and we got trounced 1–12. Them fourth years just won't run at all, I found out later they were laughing at me 'cos I was still running around, near dead, even when we were 0-10 down. They must be thick. No sense of pride them lot.

FA Cup Semi final draw: United or Boro vs Leeds at Hillsborough.

Went to Tufty Club, chep again, just mucked about with Bes, Mog and Benny. My legs are killing me."

'THE WALK OF SHAME'... Courtship behaviours evolve gradually over generations but evolve they do. There appears to be a general feeling in this post-feminist society that women hold a more involved, if not to say controlling, role in the courtship rituals. This may or may not be the case, I leave it to Germaine Greer and co to inform and advise.

One of the rites of passage we had to endure in 1970 that from my observations has changed only slightly in subsequent years was the dreaded 'walk of shame'.

This would begin with the girls forming circles on the dance floor. They would then proceed to quite literally dance around the huge piles of handbags that would accumulate. I sometimes wondered if Mick Burke the local mountaineer tragically to die on Mount Everest just a few years later, honed his craft on these mountain-sized piles of hand-bags, or *'The Heralayas'* as we called them at the time. Sometimes the circles of dancers would be many and small but often they would en-compass the entire dance floor forming an impenetrable ring of female solidarity.

Meanwhile the lads would only reluctantly dance at all. This was well before Saturday Night Fever, Billy Elliot or even the 'All-Nighters' at the Wigan Casino. It was just not 'cool' for lads to dance, certainly not in the Beachcomber aged 16 anyway. Some did of course but the majority of us would hang around the perimeter trying to catch the eye of the girl you fancied.

> This was a critical point. If accepted, a dance may ensue, if not, there was the dreaded walk of shame back to your pals

Eventually the inevitable just had to happen and, often fortified by dutch courage, desperation, or both, you would break through the circle and approach the girl of your fancy. This was a critical point. If accepted, a dance may ensue, if not, there was the dreaded walk of shame back to your pals. They would be guffawing with laughter, full of wise-cracks, whilst you would be embarrassed and angry, protesting loudly with awful comments such as, "I only asked her for a bet", "telt yur she wur a lezzy" or "it wur only for a laugh."

TIMING BEING EVERYTHING… One extension on the 'walk of shame' theme was the silent walk of shame. More common at school discos or church hall dances. Here the disc jockeys, for such was their full title in those days, were usually enthusiastic amateurs and they would frequently leave gaps between individual records. Bear this in mind.

The worst scenario involved walking up to the girl, breaching the afore-mentioned 'ring of female solidarity' in the process, asking for a dance and being rejected, only to find your timing was all wrong. To your horror the music has finished and utter silence reigns. Silence that is but for the clip-clop or squeak-squeak of your shoes as you trudge across the dance floor, shoulders drooped, face burning and peer 'cred' in the gutter. If you were really unlucky the full lights would come on for a refreshment break, (pop and crisps). It would be at this point you wished your gonads had remained in the ascended position where they belonged.

I am convinced that some of the girls, only too aware of the result-ing humiliation that would ensue, deliberately enticed me to endure the walk of shame. Perhaps this was just the fairer sex beginning to realize, not to say enjoy, the power and control they could wield in courtship behaviours. It was equally possible that this was a means of revenge for some previous misdemeanour of which I was unaware. We had quickly learned the lesson that 'hell hath no fury like a woman scorned'.

Whatever the reason it was clear that 1970 girls were fully in control in matters of public, ritualistic humiliation. Anyone who believes 'girl power' began with the Spice Girls is kidding themselves. We had our own version, the 'Spite Girls'. Oh yes, sisters were doing it for themselves even then. It was all fair-enough. After all, we lads were complete and utter prats and deserved everything we got.

February 24th, Tuesday... "Woke feeling dead stiff, legs are really sore, I must get fit! 1–12 to Shevvy? I've never been so humiliated since they made me an angel at the junior school nativity play.

School was chep as usual, Trench the Tench, our Art teacher, waited until I had finished my sketch, then told me it was too small and ripped it up. Why didn't he tell me that in the beginning? He's dense he is.

Paul and I went baby-sitting at night for a neighbour, Mrs Coates; we earned 5s which we split. We spent the night playing Monopoly with the kids then I finished my History composition for Harry Holland."

February 25th, Wednesday... "When I woke up this morning there was three inches of snow down. I was sure Latics match would be called off but it wasn't.

I did my Art work in the morning and at dinner-time went down to Latics. The pitch was dead soggy and covered in snow but it was draining off great. Korky only came into Maths at five past two so it was a pretty easy lesson. We watched the fourth years playing from 3pm onwards; when we left they were losing 0–2! They won 4–2 in the end too.

Went to Latics at night, they won 2–0." *(vs Netherfield, LFA Cup. Scorers: Tony McLoughlin and Davy Breen. Att: 1,500.)*

"We reckon Gordon Milne is a belter, best in the NPL. Man Utd won 2–1 *(FA Cup, 6th round. Scorers: Bobby Charlton and Willie Morgan)* and I watched England beat Belgium 3–1 in Belgium, played great too, for once!" *(Friendly. Scorers: Alan Ball x 2 and Geoff Hurst.)*

February 26th, Thursday... "I got my 'Charles Buchan's Football Monthly' off Sharrock at last. There's loads in about Latics. Pictures of Tony Mac, Gilly, Jim Fleming and Iain McNeill, shame they've sacked him! The morning wasn't bad but Harry Holland was in a rotten mood. Chemistry is great, phosphorous – WHOOM!! Pop was away so that was good. Pippa jumped on Woodhead's bag and then his tin of pens, knackered them he has!

The evening paper reckons Latics are definitely going to play in Russia! At night me and Paul went into town. We saw Mick Ellis, tickets for Monaco next week he says. We also liberated a stuffed fox from the props' box at St. Michael's Church Hall. We'll paint it blue and use it as a Latics mascot."

February 27th, Friday... "This morning we declared war on teacher, Ernie Piggot! He found our ultimatum and came in to call us all the names under the sun. So he has asked for trouble and he will get it!

We did our Physics practical exam today. It was pretty easy really but drawn out. We planted a seed box with plants too. Aunty Joan and my cousin David came to stay and they've brought me loads of stuff."

Although we were far from a poor family, 'hand me downs' were always welcome. Periodically my well off relatives from London would arrive and bring with them cast offs such as, on this occasion, a camera. I'd never possessed one of my own before. I was also given a brand new 'casey' football, white and pristine. Also included were fashionable clothes by Wigan standards. With striped trousers and a reefer jacket, would I look a dandy at the Tufty Club that night or what? I actually looked more like something out of the Dandy comic, "Tha favvers a butcher's boy," laughed one mate, with ill-concealed scorn.

"Me and Paul went to the Beachcomber. Val said she'd go with me but went with Clarence instead, the bitch. "I'm sorry," she says, the little get." *(So much for my flash new clothes, never to be worn again.)*

February 28th, Saturday... "This morning I went into town with Paul and bought a magazine but that's all."

"Watched Latics beat Goole 2–1. Tony Mac and Davy Breen again scoring, 2,333 on, not bad. Actually Goole probably deserved a point. There was supposed to be 400 students coming to Latics to protest *(against what, the diary doesn't say)* so we was ready for 'em, boots, clogs and everything but the mardy sods never showed up.

Went to Tufty Club at night and again there was nowt doing. Mucked about with Bes and Brocky afterwards. Crumpets asked me out again, she is 'blown em' she is, she must be!"

Periodically my well off relatives from London would arrive and bring with them cast offs such as, on this occasion, a camera

So it was that as February ended, Prime Minister Harold Wilson tried to negotiate with the all powerful trade unions in an attempt to win the forthcoming general election. Meanwhile in Wigan, Paul and I tried to negotiate with the DJ at the Tufty club to play more Jimi Hendrix and Edgar Broughton. Neither endeavour proved successful.

Latics fortunes however were looking up with Gordon Milne beginning to make an impression. At least my torture at school couldn't last too much longer, but with final year exams drawing ever closer could my life get any worse?

A ball of memories

MARCH 1970

School days, bullying and Latics 'away' games...

March 1st, Sunday... "Actually did some English homework today. Then I blew up my new football only for it to go down again. I went to Paul's in the afternoon and watched Leeds vs Crystal Palace on TV, chep it wur too. 'Top Gear' wasn't brilliant either.

Spent the night at Paul's house getting piss't on cider then went to the Tufty Club. I told Val off for the way she treats me and I might go with her tomorrow, you never know. Just mucked about with Bes 'cos Paul took off home. I am feeling rough as I write this."

March 2nd, Monday... "The writing in my diary is funny because my hands are freezing and won't thaw out! I've been out in the ice.

Morning was chep. Someone has thrown ten bricks through the art room windows. Nothing to do with me or anyone I know. It's chep is school, really rotten. The afternoon was pot too, nowt doing but dead boring. It tried to snow and there was quite a blizzard for ten minutes or so but it didn't stick thank goodness.

Beachcomber at night was pot. Shirley went with some scouse lad and Val went with France Farrell. However there is always Friday."

March 3rd, Tuesday... "It's a chep day at school is Tuesday but then every day is, isn't it? I don't understand a word 'owd Korky says but he couldn't care less. Me and Evvy went down to Latics at lunch-time. The Supporters' Club is being extended and they intend holding 'Beat Nights' on a Thursday so we'll probably go to those. Back in school we looked through the Art exam paper but it's not too bad I suppose.

Me and Paul went into town, nowt doing. Uggy, *(Peter Lester, school teacher and parent's friend),* is trying to stir things up at home about trouble at school, two faced pig."

March 4th, Wednesday... "Snowed heavy overnight again, two to three inches down and continued to snow on and off all day. We had a great snowball fight during games lesson. Best day at school for months.

Me and Paul have made a couple of posters for the Kharkov game so we put them up in town. I filled in an application form for a job at Pilkington's glass works in St Helens. My dad keeps telling me I'm wasting my time, "They'll see right through you" he says. That's as funny as he ever gets, i.e. 'never'.

Had a bath then watched Standard Lieges 0-1 Leeds Utd, chep game too."

March 5th, Thursday... "The morning passed all right I suppose. I got references for the Pilkington's job off Harry and Korky. Pop was away so we did more chemistry in Ted's. I changed my library books and pinched some blue paper for future Latics posters.

During our free lesson Keith and Woodhead were lobbing snowballs at room four. Harry caught them and sent them to Korky who as usual did nowt but tell them of his, "disappointment in them." We played five-a-side at 4pm and lost 2–6, we only had four men though.

Me and Paul went for tickets to the Monaco off Mick Ellis but he didn't get us any, daft bat. It was a raging blizzard for 20 minutes or so but then stopped.

I've bought an old RAF greatcoat off Paul for 10s."

Such attire was fashionable at the time but just what ex-servicemen thought of the idea was frequently made clear by their comments about me being "a disgrace to the uniform, you long haired hippy", or "you haven't earned the right to wear that." One old bloke, a complete stranger, even clipped the back of my head as I walked through the town centre on one occasion! All of which was water off a duck's back as far as I was concerned, after all, the more of the 'establishment' we could annoy the better, right?

March 6th, Friday... "It had snowed again during the night, about six inches in most places now. The morning came and went. I wrenched my arm throwing snow-balls, it's wrecking me now.

Pip and I went to Latics last lesson 'cos Pop's away and we were free study. They were just clearing away

the snow when we got there. Gordon Milne and Dave
Gaskell were all joining in too.

I wore my RAF coat at school; it's dead warm and fits
well. The kids in 4c kept saluting me though, cheeky
little gits.

At night Tufty Club was pot again. I just mucked
about with Bes, Brocky and Pat all night. I met a drunken
bloke on the way home; he was dead funny and kept
falling over!"

March 7th, Saturday... "More snow over-night. Went
into town with Paul and met Sayes and her pal,
'Crumpets' *(she who keeps asking me out).*"

Crumpets, was actually named Diane and was
a really nice girl. She was friendly yet rather
shy at times, especially with me although she
did possess a zany sense of humour. She was
rather self-deprecating which led her to being
the butt of many jokes. Sayes (Sue) invariably
stood up for her but even she couldn't persuade me to go out with Diane. Despite being
a typically lustful young lad, desperate for any

> One old bloke, a
> complete stranger,
> even clipped the
> back of my head as
> I walked through
> the town centre on
> one occasion!

action, anytime, anywhere, for some reason there was just no attraction
to Crumpets on my part. You see, not all 16 year-old lads have the
morals of an alley-cat?

"We all went to Latics and watched an awful game on
a snow covered pitch; 0-0 vs Netherfield. We should have
won, missed loads of chances. Man City won the League
cup at Wembley beating WBA 2–1.

Tufty Club again at night, mucked about with Bes
and Brocky. Supposed to be playing football tomorrow,
waiting for Tony Wilson to phone back but he never did."

March 8th, Sunday... "Snowed yet again overnight and
all morning but not enough to really disrupt anything.
I went to Paul's this afternoon, Goofy turned up too.
I bought Mum a Mothers' Day present, some chocolate.
If she doesn't like it I'll eat it! Goofy gave me a lift on his
scooter, strange feeling too. We watched Man City vs

WBA on TV. Good game but too many chances missed.

Tufty Club wur pot again. Val went with France Farrell again but at least she talked to me tonight, loads in fact. Mucked about with Bes and Brocky but it was chep really. Some girl phoned for me but as it was our Robert who answered the phone, we'll never know who it was."

March 9th, Monday... "I wished I'd not bothered getting out of bed today. School was pot, dead boring and no-one is willing to help us at all so they can all get lost. As soon as I get a job I'm going to go back to school and laugh in their miserable, bad-tempered faces.

Tufty Club was chep again. Paul asked Val for me but she said no so I told her afterwards that Paul only asked her for a joke. I am in a dead chep mood just now. I wish I could go back a few years."

Early Evidence of Climate Change?

It snowed in Wigan on the 2nd, 4th, 6th, 7th and 8th of March, 1970. This meant I saw more snow in the first few days of that month than I've seen in all the past few winters living in Scotland! I remain baffled as to why a 16 year-old lad was so preoccupied by the weather, particularly on non-football match days, but it was clearly of sufficient interest to record it frequently in my diary.

March 10th, Tuesday... "It was quite warm at first and the snow carried on melting, turning to sleet and rain later on. The morning passed all right and we just mucked about until Keith broke a window in the girls' school at dinner break.

Our Mark has been ill all day and still is. As I write this he is crying again.

At night I went down to Latics and saw Brocky, Ozzy, Jim Baker, and Tommy Tucker. The girls were there too, Pat is alright but nowt great."

March 11th, Wednesday... "I only got up at ten-past eight this morning, I must have turned over and gone back to sleep. I was late for school but no-one cares. I nearly bounced Evvy and will do if he doesn't shut up being such a clever dick."

"At dinner-time I went to Latics to see if the pitch was playable and it turned out it was. Then I went home for my games kit. Paul and Les, who were only visiting school for old times' sake, were allowed to join in the games lesson. We had to play on the yard 'cos the field is dead muddy.

Went Latics, at night, we beat South Liverpool 5–1! Great result, Tony Mac scored two as did Ian Gillibrand. Only 1,591 on, but not bad considering the weather of late. I've got to go for an interview at Pilkington's next week, here's hoping!"

The late, great, Ian Gillibrand

March, 12th, Thursday... "It tried to snow yet again on the way to school but soon stopped. Latics were on TV last night, it gave the result and the scorers. There was even a report in the 'Daily Express' this morning.

Grog found that bit of paper we put on his desk calling him a rat. I'm ready if he tries owt! Korky showed us some of last year's graphs exam papers so I borrowed some to give me some ideas.

I had to baby-sit at night as our Mark remains ill. So I did a few graphs and a test whilst playing records. I feel pot tonight, don't know why?"

Gidlow school remained so, so boring. The diary continues to reveal many lessons consisting of reading old exam papers or being given free time for so called 'self study'. Such spare time was usually spent 'studying' Latics' ground improvements or 'studying' the town centre.

A lot of homework involved graphs, writing mundane essays and preparing artwork, none of which was particularly taxing. Yet the teachers; Pop, Uggy, Trench, Jack, Harry, and headmaster Korky Price, to name but a few, constantly warned us of the dire consequences of arriving at exams unprepared. "You must work harder" they implored, yet gave us routine, half-hearted preparation. I did the work set before me and no more. In truth, Latics' team for Saturday was far more important than learning how to construct a pie chart. Now, if they'd asked me how many pies Latics had sold at half-time I could probably have done some research and produced an excellent pie chart indeed.

There is an irony here that readers will be quick to observe. The grammar, spelling, and sentence construction of my diary entries make it very clear that my teachers were right. I should have spent far more time attending to school lessons and less time moaning about them.

March 13th, Friday... "The morning came and went. I went into Trencher's class for two hours. I came home at dinner-time 'cos there was nothing to do at school. In the afternoon we did another two exam assignments in Ted's. They were dead easy. I hope the actual exams will be like that!

Tonight I was supposed to be baby-sitting for Mrs Coates up the road but she didn't need me so I went to Tufty Club instead. It was chep again, always is that place. When I have finished writing this entry I am going to write to 'Soccer-Monthly' and 'Football-Monthly' about Latics' game against Kharkov."

March 14th, Saturday... "Great day weather wise, sun was shining, no breeze. Paul and I went into town where

Versus Rossendale Utd

I bought a film and a battery for my new camera. Paul bought a pair of trousers. We met Sayes and Crumpets in town and went to Latics.

Good game, we beat Rossendale 2–1." *(Lancashire FA Cup.)* "They were unbeaten all season and ex-Latics player John Pearson had scored in his previous 11 games. Not today though! Jimmy Fleming scored a belter. I took some photos but missed both goals.

I wrote to Preston North End for trials today and posted my letter to 'Charles Buchan's Football-Monthly' magazine about the Kharkov game. Man Utd drew 0-0 with Leeds in the FA Cup semi-final."

March 15th, Sunday... "It was another great day today, the sun was out all day and it was hot too. I went round to Paul's in the afternoon and watched TV highlights of Chelsea beating Watford 5–1, what a bog of a pitch! We went playing soccer in the street but got too hot so we went back into Paul's house for a cup of coffee. His mum is a belter.

I went home and had a bath then went to the Tufty Club again. Guess what? It wur chep too. Saw Deano after, he's great for a laugh. Bes went with Pat at long last. I just mucked about then walked up home with Deano."

March 16th, Monday... "It's gone cold again today but at least it hasn't rained. It's probably waiting for Monday 'cos that's when Latics are playing Kharkov. We had our Art exam this morning, it was pretty easy really and we still have a lot of time to finish off the practical part. The rest of the day passed all right.

It seems that some girl from the girls' school wants to go out with me, foolish wench indeed!

The Beachcomber was all right. It was Bes's birthday and he got stoned drunk. Pat wasn't going to go with him after but we sobered him up in time. I walked home with Paul, nowt doing."

Some slight relief from school tedium was the beginning of the annual 'House Games' and the ongoing five-a-side football competition. My

House was 'Gordon' and in keeping with my downbeat life at that time, we failed to win anything of note that year. Sometimes relief of another kind was forthcoming.

> **March 17th, Tuesday...** "It was pouring down on the way to school but stopped soon after. The morning was alright; I carried on with my Art exam and found out that big John Ashall and 4T gave Ray a right good kicking during the break. Great, just what he deserved, shame I missed it. Trencher's art assessment gave me a grade 2, better than I'd hoped for.
>
> Paul and I went to Latics Club, then town later but nowt doing. We pinched a garden gnome on the way home; we intend to start collecting them.
>
> It was St Patrick's Day and a drunken Irish bloke gave us a song and a dance outside the Brocket Hotel! He was dead funny at first but then got a bit stroppy so we left him to it. Latics got a great draw away at Gateshead 0-0."

BULLYING

I imagine most schools had a bully, and ours was someone I shall call Ray. He had tormented me and my classmates for years as the class bully until his powers waned in the final year. Whilst puberty saw growth spurts that brought size, bulk and power to many lads' physique, Ray seemed to barely grow at all. Indeed by comparison he diminished in stature in every way. Those who were now bigger and more confident were only too keen to prove their newly acquired superiority and wreak their revenge. Many a long standing score was settled as the bully became bullied with no sympathy from anyone.

One morning my mate Pippa finally confronted Ray face-to-face and gave him a real pasting. Pippa had grown to be a burly young lad, but to be trounced by the previously quiet and innocuous Pippa was all too much for Ray. Humiliated and in tears in front of the entire class, this one incident was the beginning of the end of his reign of terror.

Deep down I had felt rather sorry for him, though this was buried in my subconscious, never to be acknowledged. Even then, I knew a loser when I saw one. Ray's only friends were lads he had intimidated into being 'pals'. He wasn't as bright as he thought he was and could not excel at sports without cheating or bullying. He came from a 'good' family who were relatively well off and I happen to know that his father despaired of him.

The teachers had done little to stop bullying over the years. They seemed to see any bullying as part of the toughening up process in life. It was all seen as part of 'the school of hard knocks' mentality in which teachers and parents turned a blind-eye to the misery caused. As with most bullies, divorced of his powers, Ray had nothing left. He became a non-person, ignored and despised in equal amounts.

> **Those who were now bigger and more confident were only too keen to prove their newly acquired superiority and wreak their revenge**

As a foot-note to the above, I did hear a rumour some years later that Ray became involved with hard drugs and sadly died as a result. If true I am sorry but not surprised. It is not only the bullies who are victims of bullying.

March 18th, Wednesday... "I put the gnome in our seed box in the stock room/common room. He looks very pretty! I did my Art exam piece till break, it's not bad really. We played Raleigh at dinner-time and lost 2–3. I had to borrow Evvy's boots and they were two sizes too small for me. Now I've got big blisters, they're wrecking me too.

Harry has locked the common room, the nosy pig. Paul came round at night and we met up with Sayes at Whitley High School. I left them to it and went in to watch Leeds United beat Standard Liege 1–0 on telly, chep game too."

THE COMMON-ROOM

Gidlow Boys' Secondary Modern School had not long had a fifth year. The Certificate of Secondary Education (CSE), and thus an extra year at school, was a relatively new concept. Consequently there had been no common-room. There was no hint at developing responsibility or instilling a sense of joint ownership of endeavour whereby teachers and pupils could share the fruits of their joint labour. Traditionalism ruled, in terms of teachers and pupils it had always been 'us and them'. In a laudable, if ill-fated attempt to rectify this situation, the ageing headmaster Harold, 'Korky' Price converted a stationery cupboard into a common room for us fifth year pupils. One can only imagine the powers of persuasion needed to convince his teaching colleagues of this innovation.

Not sure what to do with such a luxury and unfamiliar with the 'rights equals responsibilities' equation, we resorted to type and trashed the place. We gave the traditionalists in the teachers' camp every excuse to close the venture down. This they did with great satisfaction and plenty of "told you so's". We didn't know how to handle being treated as adults. In hindsight I suppose using the book-skip as a urinal might be seen by some as clear evidence of this.

March 19th, Thursday... "The sun was beaming down when I awoke but it turned cloudy as the day wore on. School was chep with lots of free periods. Harry wanted me to go to some Wigan Education Committee event and read out a speech. I refused so we tossed a coin for it and I won. Pip also refused to go so just Evvy went, the soft pig. Instead I went into town with Paul and booked for Altrincham away. Paul and Sayes came to my house for the evening and Paul cut my hair."

March 20th, Friday... "A beautiful day. Evvy won the Gidlow cross country, I didn't run. Went to Pilkington's for my interview, Dad drove me there. The interview went OK and there's some reet bonny wenches work there too! Tufty Club at night was chep. Paul and I went to St Michael's Church hall dance, nowt doing there either."

> The atmosphere generated by partisan fans, all combined to create a magic experience that remains forged in my memory

March 21st, Saturday... "Pouring down all day, continued all day. Paul and I went into town and I bought a pair of boots from Kay's. Cost me 10s. Had dinner in town and got on the bus for the Altrincham game.

Latics won 3–1 and Eddie kicked a big hole in the back of their stand. The coppers arrested a couple of our lads so they'll get done now! All the rest of us escaped."

Poor Eddie eventually got a right 'seeing to' by his dad. Parental corporal punishment being commonplace at the time. He was also fined by the courts and had to pay Altrincham FC for two new asbestos sheets. In a fairer world we'd have had a whip round, but we didn't, sorry. Just think on though Eddie, if you come down with an asbestos related disease you could always try suing Altrincham FC.

Despite, or perhaps because of this kind of incident, Latics away days personified all that was exciting about following Latics to away games at the time. The passion, the proximity of the players and pitch, the hint of danger, and the atmosphere generated by partisan fans, all combined to create a magic experience that remains forged in my memory. If I close my eyes, even now nearly 40 years later, I can still sense the experience. I can see in my mind's eye Gordon Milne scoring his first goal as a Latics' player (in his own net!) When I open the match programme which is beside me as I write, the smell of the printers' gloss off the pages evokes other smells such as that of liniment in the air. I can feel the chill of the Cheshire evening as the floodlights came on. The entire ground was painted red, even the snack bars (with an added tinge of blue once we'd left!).

All you veteran Latics fans can join in here. To the tune of; 'She'll Be Coming Round the Mountain'... "You can stick your Jackie Swindells up your arse – sideways!... You can stick your Jackie Swindells... repeated. Altrincham away? Oh! magic occasions indeed!

"Wigan rugby are at Wembley, chep pigs. Man United lost 1–2 at Chelsea. Tufty Club at night was all right, better than nowhere I suppose. Bes went with yet another wench. I came in and watched Man City lose 1–5 to West Ham, sick City!"

Sunday 22nd, March... "Read the papers, not much in about Latics or Man Utd either really. I did some English homework and some Art work too until dinner-time. After dinner everyone had to get smartened up 'cos Granny was coming for tea.

I went to Paul's and we watched TV highlights of Liverpool losing to Everton 2–0 and Chelsea 2 Man Utd 1. Sayes and Diane came too but left soon then Goofy came. We played footy in the street and Goofy gave me a lift home again on the back of his scooter. At night Tufty Club was chep again. Bes went with Denise, good luck to him, they reckon she's 'hot'!"

Monday 23rd, March... "Big day today, Kharkov from Russia tonight! School was OK, but Keith broke a window so we all went and hid at Latics' ground. They were putting up the flags for tonight.

It starting raining at lunch-time and carried on all day.

About 3.45pm a real thunderstorm broke and I thought
the game would have to be postponed but it turned out
different.

The rain eventually stopped and the pitch dried out
just enough to start a great game. Kharkov were superb
and were 3–0 up by half time but Latics' pulled it back
to 2–3 at the end but just couldn't get the equalizer.
We bounced a load of rugby fans who tried to take
the popular side so they are after revenge!

I have got a boil on my lip and it's killing me."

WIGAN
ATHLETIC 2

(all Blue)

1. D. REEVES
2. A. TURNER
3. W. SUTHERLAND
4. I. GILLIBRAND
5. D. COUTTS
6. I. LEDGARD
7. M. HILL
8. G. MILNE
9. T. McLOUGHLAN
10. J. FLEMING
11. D. BREEN

Other Players:
12. J. FIELDING
13. B. CAIRNEY
14. J. SAVAGE

Referee:
Mr. N. Mason, Leeds

Linesmen:
Mr. J. Higham, Wigan.
Mr. J. Cunningham,
Preston.

KHARKOV 3

A. SAVTSHENKO
V. ARISTROV
W. GUNKO
E NESMAIN
A. KAFADGY
I. MATVIENKO
B. PANKOV
A. GULAKOV
V. UDOVENKO
A. PANOV
A. BORISSENKO

Other Players in Party:
V. ZAJTSEY
N. KONOALOV
V. MARTSHENKO
A. MAIBORODA
V. PESTRIKOV
B. TRUBISHANINOV
Y. ESKIN

Officials:
W. GALUZA, Chief
V. KANEVSKY,
Chief Trainer
W. ZUB, Trainer

WIGAN ATHLETIC ASSOCIATION FOOTBALL CLUB LIMITED
Springfield Park, Wigan.

WIGAN ATHLETIC

v.

KHARKOV

at SPRINGFIELD PARK, WIGAN
on MONDAY, 23rd MARCH, 1970
Kick-off 7-30 p.m.

J. H. Tinsley, Secretary

DMISSION 8/-

The Red-Army invades Wigan and no sign of Gorbachev

If truth be told, the Ukrainians' played a brand of football that was utterly alien to my youthful eyes. They had instant ball-control and could pass it quickly and accurately to team-mates always on hand, always on the move. Rarely had I seen players able to take a 40 yard pass, kill it stone dead and pass it to a colleague, all this in a split second. Perhaps Arsene Wenger also watched USSR football as a youth? It was a similar style of controlled, possession football to that employed in recent years by Arsenal.

How the score was only 0-3 at half-time was a mystery to me and how Latics' got back into the game in the second half remains equally obscure. I think Kharkov made a few substitutions whilst we closed them down quicker giving them less time to organize their intricate triangles and wall passes. Either way it was a footballing lesson that remains fixed in my mind as to how football should *really* be played.

Emerging with a 2–3 defeat felt like a victory to me. *(Friendly, lost 2–3. Scorers: Sutherland and Fleming. Att: 3,993.)*

March 24th, Tuesday... "My lip was sticking out loads when I got up so I have to see the doctor tonight, boo. Last day at school, just as well. Raleigh beat Nelson 1–0 in the house cup, Grog got beat, great. I got a load of paper from Trencher's and a load off Harry too 'cos I've got lots of work to do these holidays.

Sayes is making a scarf for Basil Brush, our new mascot. I think she should wear it because I'll feel a prat walking round Latics with a stuffed fox round me neck. The doctor gave me some antibiotics for my boil and I am drowsy zzzzzzzz. Henry Cooper beat Jack Bodell."

March 25th, Wednesday... "No school for the next two weeks, great. My lip still hurts and is as big as ever, still very painful too. Barney Rubble and Joe Dunn came round with two LPs I've borrowed off Keith. I love Jethro Tull!

I started my geography project and managed two whole pages of it! I found a casey football in our garden, I don't know where it came from but it's mine now! These drugs seem to be making me feel rotten all the time. Paul phoned up but I stayed in most of the day. I went to Paul's later and we played street soccer for a bit but my lip hurt too much."

"Alf Ramsey named his squad for Mexico; Kiddo, Bobby, Nobby, Alex and Dave Sadler are in the squad."

March 26th, Thursday... "I stayed in all morning and did some more of my Geography project. Mark took ill and yelled all morning. In the afternoon Paul and I went into town and booked for Macclesfield away. I got a card for my mum's mate and Paul took his record-player in to be repaired. We phoned Gerald at his work and met him later when he gave us some blue paint spray for Macc tomorrow. We also met Denise who says she's finished with Bes so I phoned him to tell him, he didn't sound bothered.

My lip has gone down a load and doesn't hurt no more. Leeds Utd beat Man Utd 1–0. Had a bath and went to bed."

March 27th, Easter Friday... "Sun was shining when I got up. Our Robert went off to Scout camp without his sleeping bag, stupid twit. We had a sudden blizzard for a few minutes but it cleared up in time to go to Macclesfield.

We should have beat them 2–0 but only managed a draw 0-0. Good point though. I got a right bouncing from the 'Bollington Boot Boys'. I only managed to escape by rolling underneath a nearby coach where their boots couldn't reach me! Then the coach driver cottered me when I got out from under his bus.

Back to Wigan, went to Tufty Club, pot again. Me and Deano ran through the park hedge to escape the parky, good laugh."

March 28th, Saturday... "Slept in late and caught Paul up in Mesnes Road. We saw John Priestley in town but nowt else was doing. It rained today, always does when Latics are playing. The game wur chep, Latics right out of touch but it's a rum battle for runners-up spot!" *(NPL, vs Northwich Victoria. Won 1–0. Scorer: Turner. Att: 2,093.)*

"The rugby fans never came as they threatened to, soft rats. Man Utd lost to Man City 1–2. On a bad run just now, eh? Leeds lost at home to Southampton 1–3, what a shock. I had to stay in at night to baby-sit. Watched 'Match of the Day', Blackpool 2–1 Aston Villa. Good game in bad conditions."

March 29th, Sunday... "Chep day today. It poured down all day and never really stopped. I did get a bit of Art homework done and I got ten bob instead of Easter-eggs off Mum and Dad. They gave me a 50 new-pence-piece, whatever one them is. Just hope I can spend it.

Alf Ramsey named his squad for Mexico; Kiddo, Bobby, Nobby, Alex and Dave Sadler are in the squad

That football I found belongs to one of the Holt boys. Best give it back, there's too many of them to mess about with.

Latics are second in the league now but Macc have five games to play. I went round to Paul's in the afternoon and we talked a bit but he went to his Auntie's later on. At night Tufty Club was pot. I think I'll ask Shirley tomorrow for proper.

Got to work for Danny on Tuesday."

March 30th, Easter Monday... "Windy and cloudy but not bad seeing as it's a match day. Latics was a good game, Runcorn were one up until Billy Sutherland scored a 30 yard snorter. Tony Mac put us 2–1 up then he got another in the second half only for Runcorn to make it 3–2. Pot ref. Wigan rugby fans came after the match but never did owt, they only want Jimmy but they'll have to take us all to get him.

I have to work for Danny tomorrow, labouring, some money I suppose but I'd rather have a lie-in."

March 31st, Tuesday... "I woke up at 8.30am – stupid time. Danny came to collect me and we went working up at Ashford Rise, Standish. We shifted literally tons of earth and stones using picks, shovels and spades. I've got painful blisters on my hands and my back aches. Danny is pally with Jim Fleming, apparently his fiancée is called Isabella! It was perishing cold and tried to snow but didn't."

> "Paul and I went to Latics ground and I was about to write 'Latics' on a wall when a woman come out of her house and said she was calling the police so we ran!"

And so ended another month as my scintillating young life dribbled by in a blur of self-centred myopia.

Quite how I lived with the sheer excitement of it all is hard to understand. Surely April wouldn't see life being lived quite so close to the edge?

APRIL 1970

4-H8-032

4-H8-032-BK-2802008-2021-
09

UsedVeryGood

Mild and Bitter Were the
Days

In which our 16-year-old diarist discovers that school and exams may be better than working for a living and that Gordon Milne may just know a thing or two about football management after all.

April 1st, Wednesday... "Snowed lightly overnight and later in the morning too. April Fool's day, I was a fool to agree to work for Danny. I got to the job and it was perishing, too cold to work. My hands are chapped, red and blistered; I can hardly write this entry. Came home for lunch, Mum is ill with flu and Dad is in a bad mood.

Wasn't too cold in the afternoon and we did a good job unloading bricks and laying concrete. At night Latics beat a very young Gateshead side 3–1, we were a goal down at one point but Tony Mac came to the rescue as usual."

April 2nd, Thursday... "Had to get up early again for work with Danny Molyneux. It was very cold but not as bad as yesterday. I had to mix cement and carry bricks all day.

Mum is still ill with flu but a bit better. Working with Danny is alright really. At least he isn't bad tempered and is always ready for a laugh.

I had a bath and then Paul and I went to Latics' Club 'Beat Night,' it was great too, good ale and I got nice and merry. We were all singing "King Tony, King Tony.""

April 3rd, Friday... "Hung-over from Latics' Club last night but gradually felt better as I continued lugging bricks and mixing mortar. Had a pint and dinner in the White Horse, Standish. Glad when we finished at 5pm and Danny gave me my wages, £2 as agreed, 10s per day. Good money but he wants me to work tomorrow, he can lump it. I'm knackered.

Beachcomber wasn't bad. Paul asked a girl out for me but she said she was going with someone, so I went for a half in the Brickies instead.

Great news, Latics are almost certainly in the Fourth division next season according to the papers, great eh?"

The Chairman of the Northern Premier League, Peter Swales, claimed to be in touch with many of the Football League clubs and was quoted in the local press that; "from what I've heard it seems almost certain that Wigan will be elected." In addition Latics announced that they were to go to a full-time playing basis as of next season in preparation for Football League status. Little wonder that we fans were supremely confident that at long last we would be playing in the Fourth division of the Football League next year.

> **April 4th, Saturday...** "Paul and I went into town in the morning. I bought a record, 'Oh Well' by Fleetwood Mac but that was all. We went into town in the afternoon too and met Sayes and Crumpets. I did a lot of shopping for Mum and Dad and also bought myself a pair of football socks for myself.
>
> Me and Paul went to watch Latics reserves draw 1–1. Man Utd lost 1–5 at Newcastle! Beachcomber at night was chep but it's better than nowhere I suppose. A gang of us threatened some scousers after too."

This last incident proved to have serious repercussions for me in particular and Wigan youngsters in general.

> **April 5th, Sunday...** "I hate Sundays, especially mornings. I just mucked about the house until dinnertime. After dinner I went to Paul's and we watched Blackpool on telly. Goofy came and it absolutely poured down all day. Paul showed me loads of old newspaper cuttings about Latics he has saved, they brought back some memories!
>
> At night Beachcomber wur pot. Shirley isn't friends with me I don't think. I asked that girl again and she said she would go with me but she was still courting, tight. Still raining as I write."

> **Monday 6th, April...** "All morning I stayed in and did a load of work, mostly Maths. It's chep, dead cold out and the radio is pot in the mornings.
>
> Danny says that he can get me a pair of soccer boots for nothing, I'll believe that when I seem 'em. I carried on working and did an art painting or two but they're both chep I suppose. I was baby-sitting Mark who was feeling ill so he went to sleep in my bed whilst I was working.
>
> At night me and Paul got 'merry on sherry' and I

asked two girls but they were both courting. Bes went with Maureen Taylor!"

Tuesday 7th, April... "I only got up at 11 o'clock and just mucked about at home. I finally finished off my 'sunset' painting, looks good actually.

Danny says he's forgot my boots, I bet I'll never see 'em.

> I wrote to 'Norweb' for a job and to Latics for a trial, I know which I'd prefer

In the afternoon I went into town and took a pair of trousers to the cleaners. I bought a 'Melody Maker' and it's not bad I suppose. I went into Wigan library to read a few papers then went home.

At night Paul and I went watching the reserves draw 1–1 with Formby. We went home. I feel depressed."

True to his word Danny did eventually bring me a pair of virtually new boots. With Danny it was usually best not to ask where he got things from and so I didn't.

April 8th, Wednesday... "Last day of the school holidays. Janet, Wayne, and my nephew Anthony stayed with us last night, I don't know why. My thoughtful big sister Janet woke me up at 8.30am thinking I was late for school, stupid twit.

I wrote to 'Norweb' for a job and to Latics for a trial, I know which I'd prefer. I did so much Maths homework I got a headache. Me and Paul went for a game of soccer on Rylands. Man United 7–0 WBA Wow!" *(League Division One. Scorers: Charlton x2, Fitzpatrick x2, Gowling x2 and one for George Best. Note the attendance; just 26,582.)*

The 'Rylands' referred to above was scrub land adjacent to the old Rylands' Mill. In 1970 any spare land became a football pitch. The only artificial surface we were familiar with was turf! Many of the school pitches were either cinder based with the odd tuft of grass bravely peeping through, or wet-land bogs. It was one of the reasons I steered clear of playing rugby, the thought of playing rugby league on cinder pitches did not prove attractive to me. As one might have anticipated, the land referred to above is now a car park with the old mill scheduled to become apartments.

Thursday 9th, April... "It was snowing hard when I got up for chep school but the snow wasn't sticking. School was rotten. I've got a lot of work to do though and must stay in during the next few weeks and get it finished off.

We went to the Careers Office in town for Grog and Keith to get some application forms. They didn't like us lot in there!

> This was at a time when an off the peg gents' suit would set you back £10 19s 6d. A three bed semi-detached house was priced at £3,250

Beat Night at Latics Club was good for a laugh. No money is the only trouble. I asked Lynn to go with Jimmy but she said she was courting. Latics reserves won 7–0 against Nelson."

April 10th, Friday... "The morning at school was pretty easy really. At dinner-time we saw the King Gnome and all his gnomelets in some bloke's garden! *(In typically childish fashion we had decided to liberate any garden gnomes we found and start a collection.)*

Double Physics was alright, I don't like it but it wasn't too bad really. Pop's was dead boring and we left early 'cos of the bus strike. I saw Sayes, Judith and co walking home from school 'cos of the bus strike too, dead shamed they were!

Tufty Club at night was pot again. However, Evvy came *(Wow!)*. Came home and watched United beat Watford 2–0 on TV, third place play-off, FA cup."

This was an unsuccessful experimental play-off for the two losing FA Cup semi-finalists, only 15,000 fans turned up.

In 1970 bus drivers in Wigan earned £22 5s for a six day week. They were striking for a five day basic week with a sixth day as overtime. Just by comparison, a state enrolled nurse earned £15 for a forty two hour week and a postman £14 per week. This was at a time when an off the peg gents' suit would set you back £10 19s 6d. A three bed semi-detached house was priced at £3,250. Or you could splash out on the car of your dreams, a brand new Super Hillman Imp at £675.

April 11th, Saturday... "Woke up at 11.45am and took my shoes to Danny to mend them then watched the FA Cup final build up. A great game. Possibly the best FA

Cup final ever? Leeds 2–2 Chelsea, fantastic. Now for the replay at Old Trafford in two weeks' time. I hope Chelsea win for Paul's sake. No game for Latics but Boston got stuffed at Great Harwood 1–5, ha ha! And Aberdeen beat Celtic 3–1 in the Scottish Cup Final.

Tufty Club was chep, Maureen Taylor said she'd go with Bes but in the end she didn't. Me? I'm sick of life."

April 12th, Sunday... "Absolutely poured down all day, never stopped, spent the day doing graphs, quite a lot, too many, I never left the house. In a month from now I'll have finished all my exams, hooray!

Went Beachcomber, chep again. A band called 'Shop Soiled' should have been on but their mike wouldn't work so a replacement band called 'Winter City Garden' came on, wick they were."

April 13th, Monday... "I felt rotten at school today and yet had a good game of soccer with some juniors. Later I went down to the Youth Employment Officer but he had nothing for me.

Lovely weather today, sunshine all day. Maybe I felt really ill because it's so nice? Paul has flu he says, so he didn't go to Latics. He must be ill to miss a game. We won 1–0 thanks to a Billy Sutherland goal, a fantastic 25 yard shot too. Ref was crap." *(NPL, vs Great Harwood. Att: 2,044.)*

April 14th, Tuesday... "I got up but felt rotten so I went right back to bed again and stayed there all day. I slept through until about 3.30pm then listened to the radio, read or wrote a few poems. I felt a lot better so I got up after tea.

My Art work has to be handed in tomorrow though I've not really done very much. I did some of my Geography project at night. I'm still not right but I'm better than I was 24 hours since."

April 15th, Wednesday... "I'm a load better tonight at last. I only got to sleep at about 3am this morning! I'm worried about my exams, homework, Keith's missing record, and of course I'm still feverish."

School and exams were becoming a real concern. At last you might think, but with Latics chasing Macclesfield for the NPL title it was easy to become distracted, some things are just more important than others. At this point I had a week before the first exam, bags of time. Certainly time enough to watch the FA Cup final replay anyway!

"School was alright, I went into town in the morning and bought some bootlaces and some throat lozenges. I also got my photos back from the chemist, they're not bad really seeing as I took them.
Paul had just got up but was still in his pyjamas when I saw him. I felt piggin' rotten again at school too. I stayed in at night and did a bit of homework then watched Celtic beat Leeds Utd 2–1 on TV, great game too."

April 16th, Thursday... "Panicking now, turns out I have to have all my Art work, Maths project and Geography project in for tomorrow! I did do a lot of work at school today but I think it's a bit too late now. Paul still has flu but looks better. I went to Latics Club's Beat Night. Val came too but ignored me again. Came home and did some last minute work."

For years to come I was to console myself with the belief that being disregarded in this manner by the opposite sex was a dead giveaway that in fact this meant the girl fancied me but was too shy to make this obvious. This dysfunctional thinking provides a demonstration of rationalisation on a near delusional scale as my ego defence mechanism went into over-drive.

April 17th, Friday... "It was metalwork exam at school but those of us not sitting the exam still had to do our normal lessons, how stupid, there was only four of us! In Art I was rushing around doing stuff I should have done weeks ago, mounting and entitling them, stuff like that. While we were in Physics the two women examiners came to mark our Art work so I can only hope. Biology was chep, we did a mock exam but Keith and I had the answers in our papers!
At night the Tufty Club was chep, I think I'll ask

Judith tomorrow. Had a Double Diamond in the Brickies after, great ale."

Sadly the Double Diamond did not 'work wonders' for my schoolwork.

April 18th, Saturday... "A neat diary entry today because I've been doing my Maths project all day and that must be neat. I've finished it now however, at last! It's not bad if I say so myself. Doing it meant I missed going to see our Janet in her new house in Leyland but hopefully it's worth it. I only have my Geography project to do and then I can revise for the exams.

Home Internationals this week. England drew in Wales and Scotland won in Northern Ireland with George Best sent off for throwing mud at the ref! Latics got a great point at Boston away, 0-0. Mainly thanks to Dennis Reeves in goal apparently. Boston were top of the league until last week. Beachcomber was chep again. I didn't ask Judith, I don't think she'll go with me anyway."

April 19th, Sunday... "Latics got a great report in the 'Daily Express'... "Reeves Puts on Star Show" was the headline, big headlines too! It was a good point though.

I did my Geography project till dinner-time, I drew a big world map and then in the afternoon I did a load of writing and two more illustrations.

> At night the Tufty Club was chep, I think I'll ask Judith tomorrow. Had a Double Diamond in the Brickies after, great ale."

Went round to Paul's, Sayes and Crumpets came too. They left early though so Paul and I had a game of street soccer. We may get a team together for next season, we'll have to see. I did more of my Geography project at night."

April 20th, Monday... "I expected my 'Soccer-Monthly' to be downstairs but it hasn't come, he's a crap newsagent that Sharrock.

I gave in my Maths project to school. It's not too bad I hope, not as bad as Evvy's anyway! Geography project to be in on Thursday, I'd best get crackin'. I've done ten pages, that's all."

"We went down to Latics, no sign of the new stand they're called building and if they are going to re-lay the turf they'd best hurry up. At night Tufty Club was awful, there was only a few in 'cos there is a Beat Night upstairs in the Casino. I've cut my hand at school and it's wrecking me now and I'm tired."

April 21st, Tuesday... "It was pouring down all morning and I got soaked going to school. I'm happy though 'cos Macclesfield lost 0-4 at Hyde last night! AND... Rugby lost 4–9 at Whitehaven, ha, ha.

We mostly did revision at school 'cept in Korky's who, of course, gave us yet another graph to do. I'm frightened to death of the Maths paper 'cos I can't do owt in Maths. Did my Geography project at night and then watched England beat Wales 3–1, Bobby Charlton's 100th cap and he scored!"

April 22nd, Wednesday... "It poured down all day. We went with Keith to his house in search of a pit helmet on a nearby building site. We got soaked but no pit helmet. Then we went to Woodhead's, then the chippy. Latics' match against Skem *(Lancashire FA Cup final)* has been postponed 'cos it's waterlogged. I hope I can still use my ticket?

> 1–0 away at Goole last night. Tony Mac with the winner again, we are top of the league now!

I went to Keith's at night 'cos Paul had to do some work. We still haven't got a pit helmet. English exam tomorrow morning so I came home to revise and watched Wales vs Scotland on TV at 10.30pm, 0-0, pot too."

April 23rd, Thursday... "I was dead nervous at school today 'cos it was the English exam but it turned out to be quite easy really. The exam took all morning though. Them idiots at school won't let us all go to Hinning House now. Only six of us can go and that means us being split up so we don't know what to do."

Hinning House was, and still is, an outdoor education centre in the Lake District. Each year a select few pupils would attend for a week of fun, frolics and mayhem, some of the official activities were reputedly not bad either. The tales that emerged year-on-year meant it was a trip not to be missed. The previous year I had missed the trip because my Uncle Jack and Cousin Phil dragged me to watch Salford lose 6–11 to Castleford in the Rugby League Cup final. I only went because;

1) they had a spare ticket
2) I'd never been to Wembley, and
3) my parents gave me little choice.

At half time I recall feeling that I'd rather be at Hinning House with my school pals. I never did get to go.

> "Handed in my Geography project, here's hoping! Latics' Beat Night was good but I had to come in early to revise 'cos its English and Maths exams tomorrow.
> Latics beat Goole away 1–0, Tony Mac to the rescue again! And Macc only drew, we're gonna catch 'em!"

> **April 24th, Friday...** "It was the second part of the English exam today but I felt refreshed with the news that Latics had won 1–0 away at Goole last night. Tony Mac with the winner again, we are top of the league now!
> The English exam took a long time to do the answers but was pretty easy really. Harry Holland reckons me and Keith should get a Grade One so that's one up."

Our teacher's estimate proved to be correct, but this was one of very few successes on the exam front for yours truly.

> "In the afternoon it was the chep Maths exam. It wasn't as hard as I thought it would be. I don't think I can have actually failed, but there is another paper yet! I stayed in at night baby-sitting for Mrs Coates, a neighbour. They only came home at midnight but gave me ten shillings for it so it wasn't so bad."

A tip for anyone who earns pocket money baby-sitting, always arrange to be paid at the end of the night. A combination of guilt at being late, coupled with the effects of alcohol, invariably means you'll get paid more generously than had originally been agreed.

April 25th, Saturday... "Got up early and went to
Coppull for a pair of shoes with me dad but they had
none my size, least none Dad approved of. Met Paul and
went into town and booked for the Northwich game.
Went home only for Paul to phone saying his dad could
take us on the coach."

Having a mate whose dad drove for Smith's bus company often proved
a real bonus, and two spare seats were quickly filled by Paul and me.
After a week of exams, a breath of fresh air and real life, Latics. This
is what life was all about, away games in pursuit of the NPL title.

"Great game, end to end stuff. Tony Mac scored the
vital goal as we won 2–1. Macc lost at Boston! If Macc
drop three more points and Scarborough one, it will be
our title!!
Beachcomber was crap but I think Judith is great."

April 26th, Sunday... "I woke up pretty early for me,
about 10.30am. I read the soccer reports about Latics.
Nineteen games without defeat now, great stuff.
The 'Daily Express' had the NPL table wrong again.
I stuck all of the cuttings in my Latics scrapbook but
I've not finished yet.
    Went to Paul's and we played soccer then went
in to watch cricket on TV. Lancashire vs Middlesex,
great Lancs are too. I had a bath then went to the
Beachcomber and it was utter rubbish. Benny says
he'll lend me Jethro Tull's new album, great.
Maths exam tomorrow!"

April 27th, Monday... "We had a dead hard Maths exam
today, really hard paper just for me. I'm crap at Maths
anyway so I don't care.
    We went to Chorley at night for Latics vs Skem in the
LFA final. Chep it was, we bounced a load of Chorley
fans but Latics lost 1–2. Molyneux in goal was wick; he
let the first one in then watched the second one float
over his head! Never mind, King Tony scored again,
seven in seven games. We are at Chorley again on Sat
for the South Shields game, should be fun."

The game was played at Chorley because Latics had to replace the pitch at Springfield Park. There is something very familiar about this echoing down the years.

April 28th, Tuesday... "I woke up chep 'cos Latics lost last night and when I read in the paper that Macclesfield had won too, well that was too much.

Free period at school in the morning so we all went into Mesnes Park. We played soccer, went putting, and then watched All Saints Girls play netball. Susan Warren was there too, reet fit she is too and no danger!

Went into school later, Korky took a rare 'un 'cos he'd wanted us for Maths! Why? The exams are all over! Then big Trench tried to be hard, I'll brast him yet, if you say owt all he says is "get into class," soft dog.

At night we just talked at Paul's house 'cos it's pouring down. Big Uggy hasn't said owt to my parents about trouble at school, thank God."

April 29th, Wednesday... "I woke up chep again, Latics lost on Monday and I've got a History exam today. Woodhead came late and nearly missed it. It was pretty easy actually, rather long and drawn out but you didn't need many facts or dates etc. We went to Latics at lunch-time, and they still haven't dug up the pitch yet! They are stupid fools."

Springfield Park, Rear Stand

"FA Cup final replay at night, great game. Chelsea won 2–1 after being behind, superb. Man City won the European Cup Winner's Cup too, 2–1 vs Gornik."

April 30th, Thursday... "I don't like Thursdays, even if we've finished our exams. We did a play in Harry's called 'Look Back In Anger'. Then we was free till break. Ted and Pop's were both chep 'cos three of the class were gone for job interviews. Benny lent me 'Benefit' by Jethro Tull, it's not bad really. I took two job applications to the Youth Employment Office and then ran back to be in time for Geography.

Stew Fenton was supposed to come and fix the scooter but he didn't so me and Paul had a bash with no success. Went to Latics' Beat Night, it was alright."

The diary suggests that April 1970 was a month in which I found it difficult to prioritise life-deciding exams with all the football activities. It was clear which of the two came out on top. But... would May see this continue?

There was also the small matter of finding employment and earning some money. As for girlfriends; just how much longer could I continue to fight them off?

AN INTERVIEW WITH 'SIR' GORDON MILNE

An Interview with 'Sir' Gordon Milne

It was gradually dawning on us Latics fans that in Gordon Milne we had an exceptional manager. He had started his playing career at Preston North End before moving to Liverpool

Gordon Milne (first left), and the 1970/71 team

where he played under the legendary Bill Shankly. Gordon then moved on to Blackpool. Gordon won two League Championships, an FA Cup Winner's medal and 14 England caps.

Given all this I was intrigued as to learn how he came to be manager at lowly, non-league Wigan Athletic and what his memories of that era were. In 2008 'Sir' Gordon, as much a gentleman as ever, kindly agreed to an interview.

Whilst I am sure you get pestered by many journalists I don't suppose you are asked by many to comment upon events at Wigan Athletic in 1970?

"Not specifically Wigan, no, but I do get asked about aspects and memories from all my previous clubs. I suppose everyone has their own footballing memories that are precious to them, just like you Ken. I am still asked for autographs occasionally."

Could you explain the circumstances that surrounded your move into management at Wigan? Had you always wanted to be a manager? What made you select Wigan?

"I always admired Stan Mortenson, my manager at Blackpool at the time, and he encouraged me to think about coaching. I had many offers to coach at league clubs but just as a coach and I wasn't keen on that. I can't explain why even now, it just didn't seem the right thing to do, for me, at that time.

Arthur Horrocks was the chairman at Wigan at the time

and he knew my dad, Jimmy, from when my dad managed
Wigan. Word came to me that they were offering me the job
as player-manager and that did appeal. I was attracted by the
idea of learning management at the opposite end of the football ladder, having played at the highest level.

I felt I had enough experience to bring credibility to the job
whilst I served my apprenticeship as a manager. Of course I
was only 32 and still playing appealed to me!"

**What was the wage structure at the time for managers
and players, both League and non-league? I'm sure
readers would like to compare them to typical wages
at the time and of course to players' wages today!**

"When I first arrived I was immediately struck by the clear need
for the players to turn full-time. From a strictly football point of
view that was absolutely right but I soon realized that many of
the players earned more money with two incomes than they
ever would as full-time professional footballers, at least in the
lower leagues at that time. It did work to our advantage though,
because it meant we could attract better players to Wigan.

Personally I experienced a drop in income moving from
Blackpool. I can't remember exactly what my salary was but
I saw it as a deliberate short-term loss for long-term gain, by
starting from the bottom."

**Can you reveal any anecdotes, positive or negative,
surrounding your dealings with such players as Tony
McLoughlin and Billy Sutherland? Can you cast any light
on why Tony Mac was suspended for three months just
for playing Sunday league football or was there more to
it than that?**

"I remember Tony; he was a big lad and a talented, bustling
goal scorer. He was one who, if he could only apply himself
more, may have made it at a higher level. However Tony was
not keen on organization, training or discipline. I was always
looking to him to 'up' his personal standards. I don't remember the details of the suspension you refer to but I imagine his

anti-authority attitude may have had something to with it.

As for Billy Sutherland, he was a typical forthright Scot. He spoke his mind which I welcomed. We got on well. He was popular with the fans and scored some vital goals for us with that strong left foot. I do believe Billy could have played at a higher level.

There was a nucleus of other Scots players at the club: Jim Fleming, Davy Breen, Jim Savage, etc. Scotland produced some excellent players at that time and I was happy to have a Scottish influence at the club."

Have you stayed in touch with any of those players from the 1970-72 squads?

"Sadly not, although I did meet Geoff Davies not long ago. He is currently living and working in the USA. I was so sad to hear of Iain Gillibrand's death. That really was a shock.

My memories of Wigan Athletic in 1970 centre around people like Kenny Banks and Duncan Colquhoun; people who had their hearts in the club. Stan Jackson was always a great help. I remember I used to go down to his garage and we would sit down over a cup of tea and some toast and put the world to rights. It was somewhere for me to go and someone to share my thoughts with. Stan was a good friend and I was upset at his recent passing.

I am good friends with Jim Smith from his days at Boston Utd. They were real rivals of ours at that time. Jim and I had some real tussles on the pitch in those days and we've been good friends ever since."

I understand that you once had to buy coke for the boiler from your own pocket! Were there any similar experiences at Wigan or was it, in fact, a well run and relatively well off club during your time there?

"Yes that was true about having to pay for fuel for the boiler! We all came off the training pitch covered in mud and grime only to find there was no hot water. Someone had to pay for the coke so I did! To be fair the directors also contributed considerably. Ken Cowap, Arthur Horrocks and Stan Jackson all

put their hands in their pockets on many an occasion."

I recall going to help the groundsman prepare the pitch only to discover we only had one set of equipment! A quick whip-round amongst the directors and a trip to a garden suppliers and we were all set.

I also remember one occasion not long after I started when the team bus failed to turn up for an away game. I wasn't aware it was up to me to book the bus but it did teach me that my responsibilities were total. It was up to me to check the details of everything. I took that lesson with me wherever I went in my football career.

It was these kinds of incidents that helped forge a common bond between all of us. I really did enjoy this 'back to the roots' experience. It kept me grounded and I felt I was learning through a true 'apprenticeship' in football management. I know it was a very happy time for me and I look back on my time at Wigan with great fondness."

The teams you assembled at Wigan were arguably the very best ever seen in non-league history, the display at Man City being testimony to this. I wonder what your approach was, did you bring in players to positions, convert players to fit a system or just bring out the best in players?

"I always believed that you needed a nucleus of players that were square pegs in square holes. I believed in having good balance, good organization and a common understanding between players, management and, crucially, the fans. I had a vision in my head of what I wanted and could therefore see where we were short.

My dad (Jimmy Milne) played with Bill Shankly, and I in turn learnt a lot from him. I also learnt from Joe Mercer and Stan Mortenson. Players had to understand what you were trying to do and how they could complement each other, as a team, in achieving this."

Looking back, how would you compare top level non-league football to fourth division football at the time?

"Oh I think that some of the players we had at Wigan in 1970

could have made it if they could have applied themselves, improved their standards, and perhaps with full-time training."

This book is centred upon the life of a 16 year-old lad and the influences in his life; school, work, music, fashion, girls, football, etc. I just wondered what influences there were on Gordon Milne as a 16 year-old?

"Football dominated my life, right through school and most of my youth. When I left school I got a five year apprenticeship as a carpenter/joiner until I was 21. I would work all day then go straight off to training at Preston; no time for tea mind you! After that I was ready to just collapse exhausted into bed. There was no time for drinking, clubbing, or music. It was a different way of life then altogether. Sometimes in the summer I would play tennis and have the occasional night out in Blackpool.

I made my debut for Preston aged 16 but of course in those days at the age of 21, I had to do my National Service. At the end of the first year I was due to be sent to Malaya to fight the terrorists but I took ill with glandular fever. It saved me from having to serve in Malaya but it was a horrible experience. I felt dreadful.

This did mean that, once I was fully recovered, I could continue my National Service but in Preston. I played for the Army who had a really strong team at that time with Derek Dougan, Bryan Douglas and Peter Dobie amongst others in the side."

I think most Latics fans would agree that the teams you assembled brought great success and increased Wigan Athletics' profile nationally thus attracting better players and eventually paving the way for Football League status. Given Wigan's recent meteoric rise to fame in the Premier League, do you feel you have been given credit for your contributions? Are you, for example, a welcome guest at home games?

"I don't look at it that way at all. It was similar to Liverpool I suppose, where success was achieved by a series of managers.

I just did my bit. I feel I moved the club on a bit but I was only one link in a chain."

And yes, I have been to the new stadium. Stan Jackson kindly invited me for the first game in the Premiership against Chelsea. Dave Whelan had sent me a written invitation and I was wined and dined on the same table as some of Dave's family. It was a really good day, apart from the result, and it meant a lot to me to be invited."

It is often said that you don't pick the team you support but rather, they pick you. Given your vast experience at many clubs Gordon, whose results do you still look out for first?

"All of them, Preston, Liverpool, Blackpool, Wigan, Coventry and Besiktas. All the clubs I've been involved with. I actually enjoy watching all the football results coming in."

Were you aware that you been 'knighted' by the Wigan fans?

"No I wasn't aware of the 'knighthood' really, at least not at the time."

Springfield Park was such a vast 'bowl' of a stadium, I wonder if the players were as aware of the crowd and felt the atmosphere that we felt on the terraces?

"Springfield Park was too big for the size of the crowds we usually had. The empty terraces did sometimes work against us. It was difficult to generate the kind of atmosphere we needed with two sides of the ground virtually empty for most games."

Can you remember your first ever goal for Wigan Athletic? I'll give you a clue, it was at the wrong end!

"Er no, I don't think I can actually, when was it?" (Own goal vs Altrincham away, March 21st, 1970. Won 3–1.) "Was it really? Well that wasn't a very good start was it?"

What was your favourite ever goal scored by yourself?

My favourite goal? Well I didn't score many. Let me think, I suppose it was one I scored for Liverpool against Man Utd. It was a typically murky, wet day at Anfield, the pitch was muddy and heavy. You just don't get pitches like that anymore! Gerry Byrne hit a long shot that came straight at me. I managed to deflect it with my head into the top corner. We won 2–1 and it helped Liverpool to our first Division One Championship under Bill Shankly."

How on earth was someone of Derek Temple's fame and ability tempted to Springfield Park?

"Well Derek and I were friends and I think he was looking for something different. Perhaps he looked at me and thought, well if he can do it, so can I! We persuaded him it would be a good move and it was. It suited Derek at the time and we made sure he got good wages of course.

He was a good example to the rest of the players bringing the kind of personal standards I was keen to encourage. He brought prestige to the club of course. The transfer fee was money well spent."

Many Latics fans felt that in Gordon Milne we may just be witnessing a future England manager in the making and I know you managed the England youth team. Tell me about those days.

"Well first of all I think that our success at Wigan in the FA Cup games was instrumental in me being offered the England Youth Team manager's job in the first place. Particularly the Man City game when my players played ever so well.

I suppose I was lucky in that I had an excellent squad of young players. It was an under-18 squad with the likes of Phil Thompson, Kevin Beattie and Trevor Francis in it. We actually won the competition in Spain in 1973, winning the final 2–0 against West Germany in Barcelona.

It was partly this, and I suppose the cup games, that proved to people that I could be a decent manager and that was why I was offered the Coventry City job."

What would you say was your favourite memory of your time at Wigan?

"Oh, I think it would probably be just the sense of cama-raderie. I was learning my trade with good football folk and we all chipped in together with jobs like helping the grounds-man with the pitch. It was the complete opposite from my Liverpool days and I thoroughly enjoyed it all."

Finally Gordon, which of the current crop of UK based players really excite you?

"Well I think you have to say Wayne Rooney. He is so explosive, in every way!

Also Ronaldo who again, is so unpredictable. You never know what he is going to do next, and I'm not sure he does sometimes!

Cesc Fabregas is another I'd pay to watch, a wonderful foot-baller. But you know it's always been the same, fans come to watch great players. Preston would get a full house whenever Tom Finney played because the fans loved to watch him play."

Thank you very much for the interview and also for bringing a ray of sunshine into a young, 16 year-old lad's life and the lives of many other Wigan Athletic fans in 1970.

Gordon Milne (centre front), and the team

MAY 1970

In which...
Trouble erupts with violence on the streets of Wigan.
The Tufty Club gets even worse.
Exams are over!

Young, daft, self-centred and gloriously immature, I was ideally qualified to be a Latics fan. Exams and school took a very definite second place to events at Springfield Park. Indeed such had been the case since season 1964/65. School had long been dismissed as boring, whilst studying was a mystery. All that mattered was Wigan Athletic, terrace skirmishes, and, increasingly of late, girls, the latter proving to be as much a mystery as studying...

May 1st, Friday... "I took 'Benefit' by Jethro Tull back to Benny at school. We had a great play in Harry's, all about the war and a cockney. *('The Long and the Short and the Tall.)* We went playing bowls in the park at dinner-time. Evvy and I were losing 1–8 but we won 13–11, what a come back!

Latics have retained 'King Tony' but let Mandy Hill go, crazy, Mandy Hill is a great player! Went to Beachcomber at night and I went with a nice girl called Margaret but I don't know about going with her again even though I've arranged to see her tomorrow night."

May 2nd, Saturday... "Had to get up at 7am to go for a job application test at Norweb. It was pretty easy to start with but got progressively harder near the end. I suppose a clerk's job is as good as any and I'll be off on Saturdays to watch Latics?

Got the bus back to Wigan, followed by a quick lunch. Then back into town to get the bus to Chorley with Paul. We had a couple of pints in their club, served us easy, and enjoyed a great 2–0 result over South Shields." *(Neutral ground whilst the Springfield Park mud-heap was dug up.)* "There was a great 'Kop' and we all ran on at the end to chair Gordon Milne off the pitch. Last game of the season; we could still win the NPL! Macclesfield won the FA trophy at Wembley. I hate them lot.

Had a few drinks too many then went to Tufty Club at night, chep it were, like usual. I had arranged to meet that Margaret bird tonight but chickened out."

May 3rd, Sunday... "I tried to sleep in and get some rest but it's virtually impossible in this house. So I got up, had to read about Macc in the papers, lucky dogs. Then I tried to get the cable on my scooter but no luck.

I went to Paul's and Goofy came. We played soccer in the street on what was a glorious hot, sunny day, then went to the park. Paul came round to my house at night and we had a game of soccer in the street with a bunch of local lads. It was a good game but my legs are tired now. Later I went baby-sitting for Mrs Coates again. I like the money but it's not going to be a habit this baby-sitting thing, I'll tell her that."

May 4th, Monday... "Lovely sunny day but we were stuck in school. Pip and I went to Latics at dinner-time to watch them digging up the pitch. Gordon Milne said "Hello" so I'm dead chuffed now!

Three of us went job hunting at a supermarket; we queued up for an hour. They promised to let me know next week. I have to go for a test at Merseyside Training Council tomorrow!

Met Margaret at Tufty Club. She wanted to know where I was the other night, ha ha! I chauved Bes and his girlfriend Lorraine when I caught them snogging. Then I went home."

The diary doesn't record what feeble excuse I churned out for Margaret. To this day I don't know why I stood her up. I was later to learn that there is no worse feeling at 16 years of age than to be left standing in Lowe's shop doorway, all alone as your peers pass by sniggering as they see you 'stood up'. If you're out there Margaret, I do apologise. To be honest I was in no fit state for female company that particular night anyway. Fuelled by alcohol and football related camaraderie, it was your good fortune that I let you down.

May 5th, Tuesday... "I went to school, got my mark then went to Merseyside Training Council for a test. It was pretty easy really. Grog's dad took us in his car. It was a nice hot day again and I got back to school in time for dinner after which we went to Latics for a neb. Then I went into town where I bought a sweat-vest for 8s 11d, it's a good 'un too."

"Sayes walked down from school and stopped to chat until Paul turned up. Paul and I played soccer and just mucked about. I got a lemonade shandy from the vending machine. We saw Dave Roberts go past on the bus, dirty pig! Exams tomorrow."

May 6th, Wednesday... "I forgot to do this yesterday so I'm doing it Thursday instead. I woke up feeling rotten 'cos of exams. English Literature wasn't bad but a lot of writing, it was easy I suppose. But... General Science was dead hard, full of facts and details that I just didn't know. It was a lovely day but we had to sit exams and work all day. I cut my hair too today.

I stayed in at night and watched Celtic lose 1–2 to Feyenoord, chep game really. I started putting plastic coverings on all my single record sleeves then went to bed happy and content for once!"

May 7th, Thursday... "Piggin' Macclesfield won last night 1–0 at South Liverpool. I stayed in all morning watching the kids while Mum worked at the shop. I carried on covering my records. It was nice and hot again till dinner-time when it clouded over and started to rain. In the afternoon Paul and I went to Latics for a nosey, nowt doing.

We did find an old scooter in the Duggy, it's not in bad condition but there's loads of parts missing. At night I went to Latics Club for the Beat Night and got drunk 'cos Macc have almost certainly won the league, so please excuse the writing. I am feeling rotten now."

The 'Duggy' was the River Douglas, at the time nothing more than an open sewer. That I risked Cholera and Typhus to lay claim to a wrecked and abandoned scooter was a measure of how desperate I was at the time get 'wheels'.

May 8th, Friday... "Please excuse yesterday's writing but I could hardly even see straight! I woke up with a rotten headache and went to school. It was the metalwork exam so Woodhead, Evvy, and me played soccer. Then we went into town to look at jeans and shirts. Later on me and Keith returned and Keith bought two sweat-vests like mine. Woodhead went to Wembley so I was all on my tod in the afternoon. I just mucked about and then went home.

At night Tufty Club was chep again. All the rugby fans were in town and we chauved 'em pot in the Brickies. Could have been Latics at Wembley too."

May 9th, Saturday... "Paul and I went into town and I bought a pair of jeans, they're alreet but nowt special. Watched Wigan Rugby lose to Castleford at Wembley, on telly, great. Tyrer got carried off and only one try. Pot to watch, sick on them I say.

Piggin' Macc have won the NPL title, they got beat 1–3 but still win the title by just 0.006 of a goal, based on goal average, lucky bastards. Went to Tufty Club again. I think I'll ask Judith when I can. Chauved the returning rugby fans, gave 'em stick all night."

Northern Premier League Top Four 1969/70

	P	W	D	L	F	A	Pts
Macclesfield Town (c)	38	22	8	8	72	41	52
Wigan Athletic	**38**	**20**	**12**	**6**	**56**	**32**	**52**
Boston Utd	38	21	8	9	65	33	50
Scarborough	38	20	10	8	74	39	50

(Reproduced with the permission of the Northern Premier League, all rights reserved.)

Football League Division One Top Four 1969/70

	P	W	D	L	F	A	Pts
Everton (c)	42	29	8	5	72	34	66
Leeds Utd	42	21	15	6	84	49	57
Chelsea	42	21	13	8	70	50	55
Derby County	42	22	9	11	64	37	53

(Reproduced with the permission of the Football League Ltd, all rights reserved.)
Manchester United finished 8th with 45 points.

May 10th, Sunday... "You just can't sleep in this house, it's impossible! I got up and finished my scrapbook on Latics' 69/70 season. I've only a few more cuttings to paste in. *(Yes, real cut and paste!)*

It had been raining but brightened up later so I went round to Paul's and we played soccer and watched Australian rugby on TV. Later on we listened to John Peel on Radio One. Then about 5pm it poured down dead heavy. Paul has lent me a book about hippies, it's great.

'Review'. My scrapbook

At night I went to the Beachcomber and Bes got lobbed out for banging on the table. Barney turned up with his wench too. We mucked about in town after then went home."

May 11th, Monday... "It had obviously been pouring down during the night but it had dried up by the time I got up. I had my Geography exam to look forward to later but we were free all morning. Woodhead had a fight with Uggy, great it was. I've written a letter to Latics, now all I need is a stamp. The Geography exam wasn't too bad really but a lot of writing and loads of facts needed.

Beachcomber was chep again but it's better than nowhere I suppose. I think I'll start courting proper next weekend with any luck. My last exam tomorrow."

May 12th, Tuesday... "Oh! happy, happy day, great, superb, shit-hot day. Started off hot and sunny too, as I took my library books back. The morning went alright; we had a laugh or two anyway. The Geography exam was pretty easy but again they wanted lots of facts and figures."

95

"So why the first sentence? Well 'cos I've no more exams at all, finished, over. We only need to go school for a riot! Look out Gidlow!! I played cricket with Paul to celebrate no more exams and went in to watch Joe Bugner beat Brian London on telly."

May 13th, Wednesday... "Went sailing with the school dinghy. It was hot and sunny, we sailed, capsized, swam, and drank shandy. Then we sunbathed, capsized again, and generally enjoyed ourselves."

For some time the teachers and pupils had been constructing a sailing boat in the woodwork classes. This particular year we were lucky enough to be the first to benefit from every one else's endeavours. I think it was Orrell Reservoir that witnessed our disastrous sailing skills. However, we were very, very good at peeing in the water.

"In the afternoon we went into the park and played soccer. Grog snatched Evvy, great, he needs teaching a lesson. We had a thunderstorm for about an hour at tea-time, like a tropical storm it was, it came and went in an hour.
Paul and I went to Latics Club at night for the Player-of-the-Year awards. Dennis Reeves won it. All the players and their wives were there, reet fit 'n 'all. We all got given a free World Cup book."

May 14th, Thursday... "Pretty cloudy at first but it got hotter as the day wore on. Apparently some Macc fans bounced a ref when they got beat 1–2 at Altrincham in the NPL cup.
I went for another Saturday job at Tesco's but no luck. Spent the afternoon at school playing cards until a chap from the Youth Employment Office came to give us blah, blah, blah. I have to go for an interview tomorrow in town.
Me and Paul went to Latics Supporters' Club at night. Great, shit-hot, marvellous, superb group was on called 'Zelda Plum'. We got nice and merry."

May 15th, Friday... "Excuse last night's writing but I had a pint or five. I slept in late then went for an interview at

Merseyside Training Council. It was pretty easy. I took my Latics scrapbook which seemed to impress the bloke.

I called in to the drycleaners to collect my trousers on the way to school. I got some application forms for the Civil Service, it's good pay. We played soccer until I broke a window in room four.

Went to Beachcomber at night, Bes went with Judith so I'm sick now, but... 'this is it'."

May 16th, Saturday... "Me and Paul went into town but nowt doing, never is in Wigan is there? We met Crumpets and Janet Senior but not Sayes who was, as ever these days, doing something called 'studying'. Mesnes Park was empty so we went to Paul's and caught up with the cricket scores. Lancashire are doing great this season, they bowled Northants out for 156 and are 110 for 2 in reply at the close."

Looking back, it was interesting how cricket took over from Latics as our sporting interest. A vacuum existed that just had to be filled. This wasn't a planned decision it just seemed a natural progression. Bored now on Saturday afternoons; Mesnes Park, the town centre, and cricket took over.

Evenings remained largely centred around events at the Tufty Club or Latics 'dance nights'. Meanwhile the town centre at night, as future diary events will show, became rather more exciting.

At night I got bounced by big Mog after the Beachcomber. Me and Bes were just muckin' about play-fighting

"At night I got bounced by big Mog after the Beachcomber. Me and Bes were just muckin' about play-fighting when big Mog drove past. He thought we were really fighting and jumped out of his car and flattened me. Moggie was too busy laughing to stop his big brother from hurting me. Could have been worse, the shop window nearly went in. My head and arms are wrecking me."

May 17th, Sunday... "Mark and Clive woke us all up dead early. I was reading the papers at 10am and on a Sunday too! It was dead hot and I watered the lawn for my dad. I managed to soak Mark, Clive, our dog, Topsy, and any passers by, especially young female ones!

A mate of my dad has passed his exams so they went out boozing till late. Paul and I went to the park and met up with Bes, Mog, Deano, Sayes, Judith, etc... playing tennis, and mucking about on what was a 'Lazy Sunday Afternoon'.

We went to Tufty Club at night. 'Colonel Bagshot's Band' were on, good act. Bes didn't go with anyone and neither did I. I'm actually bored now the exams are over."

May 18th, Monday... "It was dead cloudy when I woke up but not raining. Went to school where Korky gave us a Maths lesson, why? Once he left the room we all legged it! We went to Barney's house where we had a laugh with a tape-recorder.

Went home, Barney and Keith came with me. We mucked about until they had to go back to school. I went to meet Paul on his way back from Tech. Lancashire are doing great again today.

We had some sherry at night and went to the Beachcomber. It was pot, awful. Bes and I just mucked about. I nearly bounced Brocky and will do if he doesn't belt up. Interview tomorrow."

May 19th, Tuesday... "It was dead cloudy when I got to school. We got our attendance mark then left and went traipsing through pouring rain and blustery winds into town looking for a job. We didn't get one at that. I went home and found Mum dead chuffed 'cos she's passed her driving test."

England beat Columbia 4–0! I heard the result on the radio, Bobby Charlton on the score sheet again

Paul and I contributed to my mum's success in no small way. We were kicking a ball around in the street when the ball went into oncoming traffic causing a car to undertake an emergency stop. The driver was on her test and was my mum. The examiner told her that this incident would count as her official 'emergency stop' for test purposes. Later my mum was furious with me, utterly failing to appreciate my contribution to her success. She claimed all the credit for herself which, at the time I thought was rather mean of her.

"I went to St. Helens for another interview at Pilkington's. I'm sure I saw Mog's ex wench on a passing train. I also saw some tropical fish living in a canal! Came back on the train with just married Ronnie Partington, he's a good lad is Ronnie.

Lancashire went top of the table beating Northants by 9 wickets. I felt rotten but went to Paul's and then baby-sitting for Mrs Coates again. Came home and wrote a letter to Norweb for a job."

School at Gidlow in May 1970 was a bizarre time for us fifth year 'scholars'. All our course work was handed in, exams were completed and therefore no lessons were provided, yet we still had to turn up every day. No sooner did we arrive and get our attendance 'mark' than we left again, particularly if the weather was good. We would wander around the town centre or head for the park and play cricket or even bowls. If we timed it right we would get to watch All Saints Girls School playing netball.

If the weather wasn't too good we would stay at school and play cards, or we'd muck about as only young lads can. Sometimes we'd go down to Springfield Park to watch the re-laying of the pitch or any other ground improvements. We would offer our advice to the long suffering workmen who invariably replied by asking us if we liked sex and travel.

May 20th, Wednesday... "Exactly ten days until Latics are in the league, we hope! I woke up feeling rotten, I'm sure I've got 'flu or something. School was chep, we played cricket and just mucked about. 'Nitty Nora the Bug Explorer' came but I'm OK, no bugs on me. I got yet another letter from Merseyside Training Council. I've already sat their tests!

Paul came round and we played cricket for a bit then went for a walk. Everywhere was quiet. We even went to Latics but all quiet there too, so we went to the chippy and came home. I still don't feel so good. England play Columbia tonight, I think."

May 21st, Thursday... "I didn't feel quite so bad this morning, when I woke up. England beat Columbia 4–0! I heard the result on the radio, Bobby Charlton on the score sheet again."

"Waste of time at school, we played cricket and cards then Korky showed us how to use a theodolite, some use that will be to me! We went to the chippy then played cricket through dinner-time. Grog and Popeye had a fight. We let the tyres down on a copper who came to school but apart from that, all is quiet on the western front.

At night I stayed in and had a bath then wrote a letter to an ex-girlfriend, Helen, from Melton Mowbray. Then I watched England beat Columbia 4–0 on telly." *(Pre-World Cup friendly.)*

Helen was a girl I had met on a school holiday two summers previously in Colwyn Bay. We had kept up a pen-pal relationship but, as the diary suggests, it gradually ended.

May 22nd, Friday... "Felt a lot better when I woke up. Posted my letter to Helen on the way to school. School is chep, we just muck about or play cricket. It's boring really but I have to go nevertheless. Went home for my dinner and had a rest. It's knackin' playing cricket all morning!

At night Beachcomber was rank like usual. Bes went with Judith again while Ewol and me just mucked about town again. I saw Ronnie again, oh, and Deano, pretending he was drunk, I think he probably was actually!"

May 23rd, Saturday... "Woke up early so I went back to sleep again. Paul and I went into town but nothing doing. No-one about so we watched Lancashire vs Yorkshire on TV in a shop window until the bloke came out and told us to shift. Lancashire are doing great and at close of play were 310 for 5, great stuff!

Beachcomber gets worse each week. However, me and Ewol got bounced by a bunch of skinhead scousers. The 'Kirkby Boot Boys' cornered us in the church yard and gave us a right kicking. The same gang kicked in another lad who had a lot of hard mates. He got a gang of lads together and we all chased the scousers to Wallgate Station where we got our own back. They had the hell kicked out of 'em but four panda cars and sixteen coppers stopped it all."

May 24th, Sunday... "Slept in most of the morning, awoke with a splitting headache, not surprising really after last night's kickin'. The headache soon wore off and me and Paul went to the park and played footy until a copper made us move onto Ryland's. The ball went in the bricked up pit shaft and I found some dirty magazines when I went to get the ball back.

If I write this diary with this thick felt tip pen I won't have enough space to write as much will I? Actually our Robert has nicked my pen

Tufty Club was chep again but Bes is a good mate I suppose. Apparently them scousers are after our guts. They are threatening to bring hundreds next Saturday, we'll see.

Danny tells me it's Jim Fleming's wedding soon, I wonder if Danny will get an invite?"

May 25th, Monday... "If I write this diary with this thick felt tip pen I won't have enough space to write as much will I? Actually our Robert has nicked my pen. I slept in until 11am. Got up and watched Lancs vs Yorks on TV. Yorks 121 all out in reply to Lancs 381 all out, great stuff! I stayed in all afternoon 'cos I didn't feel so good.

At night Beachcomber was chep but Val has finished with France Farrell so that option is always open? Judith nearly finished with Bes again, but not quite. Next Saturday, big day all round."

May 26th, Tuesday... "Woke up at 11am and went into town with Paul. Not much happening really so we had some coffee in Lowe's Café and came home. Sayes can't come out for four weeks 'cos of exams so Paul's a bit sick!

In the afternoon it started to rain but stopped in time for me and Paul to play cricket. Then we went in to watch Lancs beat Yorkshire on TV for the first time in thirteen years, too long!

We went to Latics and saw some plans for a new canteen and shop, etc. Talked to Phil and came home. Paul and I phoned Keith and we are going up to his house on Friday, perhaps a pit helmet at last?"

May 27th, Wednesday... "My darling little brother, Clive woke me up early with a letter from the Youth Employment Office. I went round and woke Paul up, the lazy sod! The girl at the Youth Employment Office sent me to the 'Wigan Observer' for an interview. It went well, I reckon I could get on alright there but it looks like hard work. Met Denise Mitchell and walked around town with her all morning, very nice too!

Bobby Moore has been accused of stealing a bracelet in Bogota, I've never heard of that shop! Mum and Dad took the kids for a picnic and apparently they lost our Mark but they soon found him again.

Bleached my jeans today, they don't look too bad. Lancs are doing well again, 300 for 9 declared, not bad. I met up with Bes, Mog, and Deano. We went for a walk but nowt doing."

May 28th, Thursday... "I had to stop in all morning looking after Mark and Clive but nothing much happened. Paul came round and we played cricket in the garden. We went into town in the afternoon but no-one around so we just came home. I stayed in at night and watched World Cup Grandstand, it wasn't bad. I'm writing this entry four days behind!"

> Bobby Moore has been accused of stealing a bracelet in Bogota, I've never heard of that shop!

May 29th, Friday... "Stayed in again watching the kids while Mum went to work in the shop. Me and Paul played cricket again and of course Lancs won!

We went up to Keith's in the afternoon and finally nicked a pit helmet each, a lad chased us but didn't dare do owt. We came home weary and went to Tufty Club late. Paul is fuming 'cos Sayes is being funny and not ha, ha. Big day tomorrow, Latics for the league!"

May 30th, Saturday... "And we were so hopeful too. Today was the day Latics were finally to get in the League, everyone said so. Me and Paul went into town where we watched Ewol playing cricket at Bull Hey but all we could think about was Latics. Who would be our first league opponents? What crowd would we get?

We continually phoned the ground but… no news. When I got home I carried on paint-spraying my blue pit helmet. Eventually the news came that we were still in the NPL. Cambridge Utd got in instead! So I went out and got piss't. Apparently I've arranged to go out with Janet Senior next week, it's news to me. The scousers got bounced again in town tonight."

May 31st, Sunday… "I touched up my pit helmet and it looks very good too. That was all I did all morning but we only got up late. Paul and I went in the park in the afternoon with Goofy. Judith and Sayes came too. Bes was there and we all had a laugh I suppose.

I stayed in at night and watched Mexico vs Russia in the World Cup on TV, 0-0, dead pot it was too, rubbish. Latics are going on a tour of Russia in July, great stuff! Lancs beat Gloucestershire in the Gillette Cup."

So May 1970 proved to be a month in which school gradually lost its influence on Wigan's answer to Samuel Pepys. Finding a job & earning money became increasingly important.

Latics lost the NPL on goal average by a fraction, (0.006 of a goal!) and then failed to get into the Football League, losing out to a bunch of "privileged southern nancy boys", as Paul described Cambridge United at the time.

Cricket began to dominate my sporting world on the domestic front whilst abroad it was football, with England building up to the defence of their reign as World Champions.

Finally May saw the start of a turf war with Wigan youths stoutly defending their patch against the rampaging hordes of 'The Kirkby Boot Boys', more of which in the next thrilling instalment.

JUNE 1970

Early summer saw Mungo Jerry battling it out at the top of the charts with England's World Cup squad, neither record figured in my record collection.

Edgar Broughton's march up the pop charts with 'Apache Drop-Out' ended at number 39 despite Paul and me buying a copy each. Coming up the charts fast was Fleetwood Mac (the 'proper' Pete Green 'Mac') with 'Green Manalishi'. So not all was lost in what had become a rather sterile music scene.

Edgar Broughton Band
march up the charts

June 1st, Monday... "Had to go to school today. We mucked about and played cricket until the ball split in two. I went home at dinner-time with Keith and Evvy and gave Keith his Jethro Tull records back. Mum went into town so I had to baby-sit our Mark.

Beachcomber was bloody awful again. The only good thing was after it closed watching all the skins in town fighting the greasers. Great it was, coppers everywhere with dogs and all. Went home tired, but not sleepy."

June 2nd, Tuesday... "I was ready to go school when Danny called asking me to work for him. So off we went to Ince where we bricked up some windows in a derelict pub. Danny, the stupid git, threw a metal bucket from an upstairs window hitting me in the face. I'm all cut up now and look well! I've got a black eye and busted nose. All Danny was worried about was the mortar going off and me getting blood on his precious timber!"

"Some girls working opposite were teasing me. One of them asked me out but she wur far. Danny shamed me pot shouting things like "Kenneth, what you doing over thur with them slappers? I'll tell tha Mother."

After work Paul and I went in the park and played cricket then went home to watch England play Rumania in the World Cup. It wur 0-0 at half time when I went to bed but England on top."

June 3rd, Wednesday... "I couldn't sleep last night at all. I listened to the England game on my radio in bed. We won 1–0, Geoff Hurst scoring. It was about 4.30am before I got to sleep.

When I got to school there was only Barney and me there so we sun-bathed in the park and then went to Paul's. We left at 12 o'clock and went home. I phoned for an interview at a paper mill in Horwich. Me and Barney went to Wigan baths and left about 3pm.

At night Paul stopped in studying so I met with Bes, Mog, and Deano and went to look in the baths. I began to feel rotten so I came home to watch Italy vs Sweden on TV."

June 4th, Thursday... "I'm writing this late 'cos I felt so ill I couldn't see, never mind write! I went to school feeling rotten and gradually got worse. In the afternoon I was even worse but went to Horwich for an interview. It wasn't a bad job I suppose but shift work, that's the snag.

I came home feeling a bit better but it worsened again. At night I felt OK and went to Latics Club but came home early. Mum has cut her thumb on a carving knife and has had to have stitches."

June 5th, Friday... "I woke up a different lad! A good night's sleep did the trick and I felt great all day, Mum reckons I must have caught the sun.

At school we played cards or cricket, sunbathed and just generally mucked about. I came home at dinner-time and decided to stay off all afternoon. I helped Mum around the house 'cos of her cut thumb then had a bath and went to Paul's at 4pm."

"At night we went to the Beachcomber again. When we got there Judith was crying 'cos Bes had finished with her. She asked me to go with her so I am doing, and quick, eh what! I'm working with Danny all next week too, boo!"

As an interesting aside, Wigan Rugby League Club, considered by many ill-informed folk at the time, and since, to be the only sporting club in Wigan, were facing a crisis. So poor were their home crowds that they considered playing their games on a Friday night. Despite winning the Lancashire Rugby League Cup and reaching Wembley, the average home crowd was a miserly 8,461. So much for Wigan always being a 'rugby' town.

> The ongoing ill-feeling between the local Wigan youth and those from Kirkby continued throughout the summer

June 6th, Saturday... "Paul and I went into town in the morning, both of us with colds. Paul bought a T Rex single for 2s 6d and the new 'Free' single. *('All Right Now')*. We went home and played the new records then I went back into town and bought 'American Woman' by Guess Who. It's great.

Saturdays are boring in the summer. We went to Wap's house for some cheap sherry and then went to the Tufty Club. Judith promised to go with me tonight but went with another lad instead, the bitch. A lad got axed in town and there were ten police dogs and police vans roaming the streets."

The ongoing ill-feeling between the local Wigan youth and those from Kirkby continued throughout the summer. British Rail were considering banning people they described as 'yobs' from their trains between Liverpool and Wigan, this after they ran riot on what was dubbed 'The Skinhead Special'. The Kirkby skinheads were reported by the local press to have been "terrorising passengers using obscene language and insulting behaviour." These young lads gloried in the name of 'skinheads' or 'bovver boys'. They shaved their heads, wore T-shirts and braces and finished their uniform off with heavy duty boots. They were the street fashion fascists of their time.

Gangs of less than a dozen would travel separately to avoid alarming British Rail authorities. They would then gather in Wigan town centre where the local youths, of which I was one, were only too happy to accommodate their invitations for 'bovver.' Now I didn't mind the occasional dust-up, but with painful memories of the beating on May 23rd still fresh in my mind, I tended to pick my moments to show off what little bravado I had. This usually involved situations where we outnumbered the Kirkby boys by at least four to one. 'You can't be too careful,' I though to myself at the time. Bear in mind I also had my stunning good looks to consider.

My caution proved justified when I learnt later that one of the gangs from Kirkby arrived at the Beachcomber armed with a gun! It turned out to be an unloaded starting pistol but we weren't to know that, were we? It is sobering to reflect that in this current gun culture climate, the gun carrying 'bovver boy' would almost certainly have carried an actual, loaded gun. Equally disturbing is the thought that he would have had every chance of being shot by a police marksman whether the gun was later identified as being an empty starting pistol, or not.

Back in June 1970 however various skirmishes would occur with cuts and bruises equally traded. Occasionally these fracas would turn into a much larger affair with upward of a hundred youths involved. Many would be high on a cocktail of alcohol, adrenaline and raging testosterone. All would be fully charged up and raring to go for an all out war.

One Saturday night the Kirkby boys were rounded up and put back on the 9.30pm train to Liverpool from Wigan Wallgate

Eventually the police forces of Merseyside and Wigan decided that 'enough was enough' and took a firmer line. One Saturday night the Kirkby boys were rounded up and put back on the 9.30pm train to Liverpool from Wigan Wallgate station. This operation gave us the opportunity to witness police crowd control methods of the time. These were, to say the least, interesting. Looking back I am fairly certain that this was the type of situation where Detective Inspector Gene Hunt acquired his attitudes and learnt the skills of his trade.

As I recall, the tactics involved the police herding the skinheads into a corner from which there was no escape, the railway station ticket barriers on this occasion. They would then launch a series of attacks with batons raised. Dogs and horses dealt with any would-be escapees. I was a likely looking miscreant myself, not that I dressed as a skinhead at all, but I still had to be careful. This was one of those situations in which the police literally took no prisoners, the cells having already been filled. If you got too close to the action there was every chance of ending up being cracked on the skull with a baton or even worse, being forced onto a return train with a bunch of very angry Kirkby Boot Boys. It didn't bear thinking about.

Rumour at the time had it that this is exactly what happened to one young Wigan lad. Thinking on his feet, he mustered up the best scouse accent he could manage throughout a seemingly endless journey and then waited until the Kirkby boys had all alighted before promptly giving himself up to the police for a return trip to Wigan.

June 7th, Sunday... "It has hardly rained for three weeks and everywhere is dry and dusty. I read until dinner-time and after lunch went round for Paul. We went into the park, the weather is sweltering. We played soccer for a bit then just sat and talked until 5 o'clock.

I watched England lose 0-1 to Brazil but we could and should have won it. Geoff Astle missed a sitter, so did Bell and Lee too.

Went to the Beachcomber about 9pm but it was chep, came home feeling rotten. Apparently I'm not working for Danny next week after all, daft sod." *(Oh yes I was.)*

June 8th, Monday... "Woke up feeling rotten but it soon passed. It was dead hot and sunny again and we just played cards and mucked about at school. We went to the park but it was dead so I just went home for my dinner. After, I found Paul and my mates all playing soccer in the park but they finished just as I got there! We mucked about and then went home.

Beachcomber was chep. Judith didn't go so, 'tits' to her. I have to ask Maureen Taylor for Bes tomorrow."

June 9th, Tuesday... "It was boiling hot again today and dead boring again too. At school we just played cricket and cards all day. If we sunbathe we get too hot and sweaty. I bought three Jubilees today! I also asked Maureen Taylor for Bes, she and I spent the whole afternoon talking. If Bes wasn't so keen I'd ask her for myself, she's dead nice.

At night Paul stayed in so I called for Bes and we went to meet Maureen Taylor but she'd left. We saw her later and talked for ages."

June 10th, Wednesday... "Danny picked me up at 8.30am and we went to work building an extension on a house in Standish. It was red hot, it has been for weeks and everywhere is dry and dusty. I got sunburnt mixing mortar and lugging bricks. It wasn't too hard work but hard enough.

Got a letter from Helen. Paul stayed in studying but me, Bes, and Mog went into town where we mucked about doing nothing. No papers today, they're on strike. Watched Brazil vs Rumania in the World Cup. Hope Brazil play England in the final now."

The World Cup, hosted by Mexico, was not the high impact, 'in yer face, can't avoid it if you tried,' affair like the present. Most games, though not all, were on late at night as I recall, with grainy black and white pictures and dodgy action replays. Colour TV was available to those who could afford to buy a colour TV set. Sadly the Barlow family was not so affluent.

What I remember most was the incredible heat the games were played in. You could see the mirage-like thermal waves shimmering off the crowds and the pitch. I do remember *that* save by Gordon Banks against Brazil. We 16 year-old experts felt that England winning the World Cup again was a virtual certainty with only Brazil likely to get in the way.

June 11th, Thursday... "No papers again today, they're on strike! Danny picked me up and we worked at Standish again. We did nothing all morning, just drove around looking for buckshee concrete. We found some and laid it in the afternoon and did a good job considering I had never done this sort of thing before.

I had to have a bath when I got home and then watched 'Top of the Pops'. Our Clive got a bike and a toy tank for his birthday. I wrote to Adele and cleaned my bedroom a bit. There was a belting film on but I left it at 12.30am, too tired."

June 12th, Friday... "Danny picked me up at 8.15am. We picked up odds and ends at the builders' merchants and then went up to Standish. We were just bricklaying but it's hard work carrying bricks and mixing mortar all

day long. I have got a lovely suntanned back. Went home
and had a nice cool bath. Danny gave me £3, that's £1
per day, not bad.

Beachcomber was chep, Bes went with Judith again,
swine. Sayes was on holiday at the Lake District. Me and
Paul just mucked about and came home. I am very tired,
well and truly buggered!"

Danny Molyneux, 'Master Builder' of Beech Hill, Wigan, taught me a
lot, most of which would not appear in any building manual. A loveable
rogue, Danny knew more tricks than Paul Daniels. If there was a
quicker and cheaper way to get the job done
that still remained within the standards re-
quired, he would do it.

In the Britain of 1970 times were hard in
the building trade. Home improvements and
DIY had not yet been promoted by TV programmes to the point whereby folk believed
that loft conversions, conservatories, kitchen
extensions etc were absolute essentials to a
life of consumerist bliss.

> We 16 year-old
> experts felt that
> England winning
> the World Cup
> again was a virtual
> certainty with only
> Brazil likely to get in
> the way

Laurie Barratt was just starting his home building empire. The
building boom was in its infancy and certainly had little effect on your
average jobbing builder like Danny. With a family to raise Danny made
money whenever and wherever he could.

One trick he employed was to have me lie in the foot well of the
van as we entered the builders' yard and across the weighbridge.
I would then get out of the van and sneak beneath the vigilant eyes of
the guy operating the weighbridge when we left. This ploy allowed
Danny to pocket the difference in materials.

Following concrete mixers around was another common trick. The
idea was to find a driver who had enough concrete left in his wagon
for our purpose but not so much that it was worth his while returning
it to the depot. A few quid would change hands and the concrete
would arrive, usually with no notice and at a time that suited the driver
and not us poor sods who had to lay it. This was usually very late in
the day.

Danny was, and still is, a good builder. He has always been an
excellent brickie with a good eye for style, impression, and attention to
detail. More importantly to me at the time, he was good fun to work
with and didn't believe in working himself, or me, to exhaustion.

'A good day's work and no more,' was his motto. I am pleased to say that he is still in demand as builder. Although in his seventies, Danny paces himself even more gently these days. He also continues to do all he can to sustain the brewery trade in Wigan, which, in these days of recession, is very civic-minded of him.

> **June 13th, Saturday...** "Our Mark woke me up dead early, about 10am so I had to get up; he pesters me until I get out of bed. I had £3 wages to spend so I went for Paul who wasn't in. I then went into town and met Ewol who bought a pair of training shoes. I bought a load of stuff for our Clive's birthday party. Every month it's someone's birthday in our house.
>
> Met Paul and we went to buy a denim jacket but they were too big. Mucked about with Barney in the park then went home. Went to Paul's and had some sherry before going to the Tufty Club or 'Rave Cave' as some call it now. It's Sayes's birthday today. I had a pint in the Market Hotel before going home, bored."

Paul had a friend whose dad owned a chemist's shop. This offered a ready supply of sherry, apparently used in making up some of the medicinal concoctions. We were able to obtain bottles of said sherry and, believing it to be an innocuous drink for old ladies when the vicar called, gulped it down with great relish. This was rough stuff though

Two rogues casing the joint, Latics' Supporters Club. Ewol & Paul

and very powerful. Once we taught our palettes to ignore the taste we also taught our livers to metabolise the foul stuff. In addition we weren't au fait with the etiquette of drinking sherry from small glasses whilst cocking the little finger; we drank it in half pint glasses. Is it any wonder that Paul claimed to see a ghost after one such session?

June 14th, Sunday... "Woke up at 10 o'clock and read a book or mucked about until dinner. I wrote to Latics for a trial too."

"Me, Paul and Derek watched cricket on TV then went to the park. We had a good game of soccer and just lay around having a laugh or talking. I went home to have my tea then watched more Lancashire vs Essex on TV before turning over to watch England lose to West Germany 2–3 in the quarter-final of the World Cup. They were 2–0 up too England! They deserved to win but didn't so it's cheddar I suppose, that's it, we're out.

I have to work with Danny again next week, chep."

June 15th, Monday... "Woke up depressed 'cos England are out of the World Cup. That Bonnetti is a pot keeper. Danny picked me up at 8.30am and off we went to Standish again. It's not too bad once you get used. Mum, Mark and Clive came to have a nosey. We have nearly run out of bricks but finished at 5.20pm. Came home and had a bath.

Beachcomber was chep again, we just talked. Mog nearly got bounced by Johnny Ras, being cheeky as usual. I've had bad toothache all day and it's getting worse. Came home feeling rotten."

June 16th, Tuesday... "I woke feeling rotten 'cos of my tooth ache. Danny took us up to Standish but we couldn't work there 'cos he couldn't get the right stuff. We went on to another job in Parbold digging drains.

My tooth hurt all day and every time I bent over to dig out the trench it felt like my tooth and jaw would burst open. I didn't do too much and Danny was not impressed when he came back from wherever he vanishes to.

Came home to find a letter from Cooke & Nuttall's paper mill in Horwich to say that I start next Monday!

Went for Paul but he was staying in studying again so I met Bes and we went in the park, then to Sacred Heart Youth Club, then on to Latics, then came home."

June 17th, Wednesday... "Danny's wife, Margaret, had a baby boy last night, they've called him Darren. This meant Danny was late picking me up. I'd hoped I'd get the day off but no chance with Danny. We went to Burscough and picked up some window frames for the job at Standish. It's looking good now; we'll have the roof on soon.

My toothache was murder again until I got home and took some pills. They did the trick and I went to the park playing soccer with Oggy, Jimmy Baker and Tom Berry. When I got home Mum had a 'clothes party' so I read a book in my bedroom till they had all gone. Later I watched Italy vs West Germany, World Cup semi-final, 1–0 at half-time when I went to bed."

In going to bed early I missed a classic game of football. This World Cup semi-final will go down as one of the greatest games ever played at this level with Italy finally winning 4–3 after extra time, going on to play Brazil in an equally classy World Cup final.

June 18th, Thursday... "I woke up feeling a lot better. Danny and I went to a woodworks up Marsh Green way. We went on up to Standish and started to put the roof on the extension. It's not so bad at all now really. I didn't do too much 'cos Danny was away for so long.

My toothache returned later on but I had a bath and went to Latics Club to see 'Zelda Plum'. It went great; they are shit-hot, a good night. Came home and watched the general election results on TV until 12.30am."

June 19th, Friday... "Ted Heath has won the general election. Bit of a shock but my dad is pleased apparently.

My tooth still hurts but not as much. Danny and I did the roofing up at Standish with boiling hot pitch. It was dead hot today but my tooth kept nagging me and I can't enjoy the weather. Danny and I went for a drink after work and he paid me £5!"

"At night Beachcomber was pot again. Me and Paul aren't going to the Monaco now 'cos Sayes won't go!"

It was on one of these occasions whilst working for Danny when, presumably seeing it as part of my education in life, he showed me something I have never seen before or since. Well, once on TV recently but on the basis that you can't believe all you see on TV, I don't count it.

I don't recall which pub Danny had dragged me to kicking and screaming. "No, no, Danny, let me carry on working while you drink in the pub." But no, I had to go with him. He couldn't let me work unsupervised, health and safety rules, you understand. Danny bought me a pint and told me to sit in the corner and be quiet, as was his want. He promptly vanished only to return a few minutes later asking me for five shillings, something I politely declined. But Danny was insistent, "Kenneth, you'll never see owt like this again, it's worth five bob I promise thi."

This World Cup semi-final will go down as one of the greatest games ever played at this level with Italy finally winning 4–3 after extra time

Danny was adept at getting people to part with their cash. Card tricks, stunts on the dart board and duff quiz questions. One example of the latter being, "Who was the only England captain to tour down-under but never got to bat?" Danny's answer, having taken your money was "Captain Cook."

I was therefore understandably wary but this was different. I could see other men putting in their money. I was also aware that this was seen by Danny as part of my initiation into the world of the working class 'Wigginer', a rite of passage, and anyway, I was intrigued.

When a sufficient amount of cash had been collected the show began. A chap called Mac promptly sat down and put a pint glass to his mouth. He cracked the lip of the glass into smaller parts, then to my astonishment and horror, crunched them in his teeth until he slowly but surely ate every bit, except the base. I was certain that there was some trick to this. I was equally aware that if there was, a pub full of angry work men was not the place to pull such a deception and hope to leave alive, especially with a gut full of fresh glass.

It transpired that Mac, Bernard Malcolm Graham aged 33, from Gathurst, was a regular on the pub scene where his glass-eating talents must have earned him a tidy income on the side with little apparent harm to his health. "I wonder what he uses for bog paper?" mused Danny, as we left.

June 20th, Saturday... "I woke up with the same splitting headache I went to bed with. So Ted Heath won an election, so what? England are out of the World Cup and there's no Latics to go to, I know what's more important.

Paul and I went into town where I bought a pair of white pumps and a shirt, 'Mr Money' me now! Me and Paul played cricket in the garden and then went to Bull-Hey to watch Wigan Cricket Club who played pot.

Mum, Dad and the kids are all at Southport with the Beech Hill Labour Club outing. Beachcomber was chep, I really must go with a girl soon, I'm getting a bit cheesed off being alone."

June 21st, Sunday... "I woke up about 10.30am and just read a book. Me and Dad went to get a garden swing from Mr Mayo, our neighbour. We put it up in our garden for Mark and Clive.

Me and Paul went to watch St Michael's at Walking Day and then went up to the park. Sayes, Judith, and Dianne came. We laughed at Dianne and talked all afternoon. I think Judith is great, I wished Bes would finish with her!"

> I don't know why but I feel depressed and wished I'd not been born, as I often do

Judith was small in stature but, like so many small people, large in personality. She was bright, funny, sassy, and at times quite feisty. She had an instantly appealing face with an impossible to control fringe that she found exasperating, but which I found strangely alluring. I liked Judith a lot, but deep down I always knew that she only had eyes for Bes.

"I watched Brazil beat Italy 4–1 to win the World Cup, good game and Brazil deserved it I suppose. I tried to cut the wart off my finger but didn't succeed, hence all the blood on this diary entry."

June 22nd, Monday... "The alarm went off at 7am. Had my breakfast and walked into Wigan to get the bus to Horwich to start work at Cooke & Nuttall's."

Two of my weakest subjects at school, and ones I had no interest in whatsoever, had been Physics and Chemistry. To this day I don't know why I applied for a job in the laboratory of a paper mill. Even more unlikely was the decision of the interviewers to give me the job. I long suspected that my dad, fed up with me loafing around, had some influence in their decision. A friend in senior management maybe?

"The job looks easy or will be when I get the hang of it. I had to measure paper, then weigh it and put it on a special machine that bursts it and measure the PSI reading, easy as that! They are nice lads to work with too. They let me leave at 4pm 'cos it was my first day. It poured down in sheets and I got soaked on the way to the bus stop.

My first day in a proper job and so I went to Tufty Club at night to celebrate. Pot again it wur. Gray Woodhead came but Paul didn't. I think I'll ask Shirley soon too."

June 23rd, Tuesday... "I got up, had my breakfast, walked into town and caught the 8.15am bus to Horwich. I seem to have the hang of what I've been taught so far and it's pretty basic. I had to actually join in with the lab-team in the afternoon because the paper-tester didn't turn up. I cut my finger very badly but it has healed up well. I caught the 6 o'clock bus back to Wigan and called in for Paul who is studying for his exams so I just came home and read a book. It's called 'Pied Piper' by Neville Shute and it's good too.

I don't know why but I feel depressed and wished I'd not been born, as I often do."

June 24th, Wednesday... "Poured down all day today. The same old routine, got up, rushed breakfast, hurried out to get to work. It isn't bad I suppose, the job I mean. It's great at work but knackers your feet and legs. I'm beginning to get the hang of things now and in a few months or even weeks I'll be alright. I have to work 2 till 10pm tomorrow but at least I can have a lie-in for once.

In the evening me and Paul played soccer in the park until the parky stopped us. I'll write a letter to Helen now 'cos I got a reply from Latics inviting me for a trial so I'm in a good mood!"

June 25th, Thursday... "I slept until 9am 'cos I'm on shifts for now.

Paul and I went to the park office but there was no-one about so we went into town. Paul got a magazine and we saw Les Ritchie doing his maths exam in the Tech. Hope we haven't put him off!

I bought some chips then took my trousers to the dry-cleaners and finally ate my dinner, before getting the bus to Horwich again. I'm working with a lad called Dave Challander who is great to work with and intends to go to Bath Festival this weekend, lucky dog! Got the 10 o'clock bus back to Wigan. Came home and watched Woodstock on TV."

June 26th, Friday... "Haven't I written a lot on these two pages? I got up about 10am and Paul and I went into town where I bought a flask for work from Whelan's. I then went home, made my dinner and then made my butties for work. That lad, Alan was at the bus stop so we caught the same bus. He works at my place, on the line somewhere.

I was allowed to leave at 5.30pm and was ready in time to go to the Beachcomber which was chep again. I think I'll go the Blues Night at the Park Hotel next week instead.

Paul can work for Danny next week, sick on him!"

June 27th, Saturday... "I only woke up at 11 o'clock and Paul had already gone into town. I met him on the way back and we tried to phone Latics to see if it was true that Tony Mac was really leaving? We couldn't get through. I got in to watch Rod Laver beat Roger Taylor at Wimbledon.

I went round to Mrs Coates' baby-sitting for an hour before going to the Tufty Club with my earnings. It gets worse each week that place. Sayes had a very nice dress on. It didn't leave much to my imagination anyway! One of her mates came who is daft as a brush but good for a laugh."

June 28th, Sunday... "Great morning, everyone slept in until 11.30am, even the kids!

I went round for Paul and Derek was there. We all went to the park but it was pot. I still wish Judith would finish with Bes so I can go with her.

There was a great group on at Tufty Club at night. A bunch of gypsies came too! They were dead far and awful dressed. I just mucked about with Benny after and then went home. I'm sick of not going with a girl and must make amends soon."

June 29th, Monday... "Got soaked on the way to work again. I met the third shift today; they seem alright but a bit old, mostly in their thirties. I don't like the canteen staff, they seem to have it in for me as the new lad, don't know why but to hell with them. The whole afternoon passed quick with Kev Pearson and Dave Challander, these two daft lads I'm working with. They are both quite mad, just right!

Beachcomber was chep, chep, chep and chep, it gets worse each time. Pat Waters is very nice though, I like her so if I play my cards right, who knows?"

June 30th, Tuesday... "The chap across the road gave me a lift into town today and I bought some magazines before catching the bus to work. It's pretty easy now but there is a chap coming next week to see if I'm working alright. I helped David with some experiments in the main lab this afternoon which are important apparently.

> Although popular with girls, I lacked the confidence to take matters beyond friendship and flirting.

It poured down and I got soaked again coming home but I dried out and went round to Paul's with my £1 deposit for my holidays in Bournemouth. We just talked and Paul lent me some horror books to read."

So June has seen my love life limited to say the least. Although popular with girls, I lacked the confidence to take matters beyond friendship and flirting.

Latics barely rate a mention in the June diary. Rumours that Tony McLoughlin was to leave were of course too ridiculous for words. He left, and to Altrincham of all places. On the positive side there was only July to get through and a new football season would start, and what a new season it would turn out to be for Wigan Athletic.

June 1970 proved to be very much a transitional period in your humble diarist's life, finishing exams and leaving school, starting work and making new friends and colleagues.

It should have heralded bright, exciting new horizons, but guess what?

JULY 1970

Which proved to be a month of cricket, holidays, and life-changing news.

'Twas July, in the year of Our Lord 1970, and in Wigan, things were coming to a head. Disparate elements were bubbling up nicely together with a whiff of brimstone and treacle. But enough of my mother's kitchen.

Life for your diarist was rapidly changing. At a time when the football close season meant my obsession with Wigan Athletic had to be somewhat suppressed, other less important matters; such as work, girls, music, and holidays all came to the fore.

> It was pay-day today and I got my first full pay packet! £7 0s 7d but I earned £8 0s 1d so work that out?

Just to set July 1970 into a musical context, this was the month in which the pop charts included the Kinks with 'Lola', Ten Years After with 'Love Like A Man,' and Free 'All Right Now'. That may sound pretty good but do bear in mind that the charts were also infested with Shirley Bassey, Cliff Richard, Glen Campbell, and Pickettywitch. Not quite so impressive now!

Elsewhere, in golf Jack Nicklaus won the Open, the Aswan Dam in Egypt was completed and a state of emergency was declared in the UK in response to the national dock strike. July 1970 also saw trouble escalating in Northern Ireland.

July 1st, Wednesday... "Went to work again and bought a paper on the way. It's pretty easy at work now I've got the general idea and everything goes pretty smoothly. I don't like the dinners because they're too much like school dinners for me. The lads on the afternoon shift are great to work with and are good for a laugh. The bus home leaves at a different time each day, it is so stupid.

At night Paul and I phoned our hotel at Bournemouth and then went to Latics' to see the terracing being constructed, it's coming along."

July 2nd, Thursday... "I got soaked again on the way to work and it poured down all morning. It was pay-day today and I got my first full pay packet! £7 0s 7d but I earned £8 0s 1d so work that out? Daft me has agreed to help-out and work on Saturday so even though I've now got money, I can't buy owt. I played cards at dinner-time

125

with some lads off the production line who thought I was
a bit left out of things.

I missed that stupid bus again so I only got home
late. Paul and I watched telly in his house and then
I went home for a bath. This job is OK but you do need
good workmates to relieve the boredom. Kev is usually
good for a laugh."

July 3rd, Friday... "I got up at eight o'clock and had a
good breakfast before I caught the 8.45am bus getting
to work at ten past. The mornings go quick and so do
dinner breaks when I play cards with those daft nits.
I helped David do some dying in the main lab and now
my hands are covered in dye.
It won't come out either.

These dumb buses make me sick,
I only got home at five to seven and
I left work at five o'clock! I just
had time to get changed and go
to Paul's when I saw him going down
the road. Tufty Club was pot again.
We saw a load of folk off on their
holidays, mostly to Newquay, lucky dogs."

> I met Bes and we
> went shopping.
> I bought a pair of
> 'Huskie' jeans in
> the sale. Bes got a
> Ben Sherman shirt
> from CD

July 4th, Saturday... "I got up at 5.45am and went out in
a horrible drizzle to catch the bus to work. It was alright
at first but as the day wore on it got rather boring and
very tiring. Kev isn't too bad to work with I suppose.

Tufty Club was bloody awful again, rubbish actually.
If only Sayes would go somewhere else but she only goes
where SHE wants to go. I had a drink with Bes and just
mucked about before coming home well and truly
knackered."

July 5th, Sunday... "I got up about 10.30am and just
read a book until dinner-time. Keith came round on his
Honda 50, it's not bad really.

I went round for Paul and met Goofy who was already
there. Me and Goofy went to the Park 'cos Paul was going
with Sayes for a romantic walk to Haigh Hall. Nowt doing
in the park so we went up Haigh Hall too. We managed

to avoid the two love birds but did meet Ewol, Ozzy, Mick and some of Derek's mates. We mucked about and had a reet laugh dodging the parky, grumpy owd get!

Later on I went for Paul. We played cricket in the street, talked and watched TV in his house until 10pm.

Mum and Dad think prices are the same now as five years ago when our Janet was buying things, they just don't understand."

July 6th, Monday... "Work gets a bit boring sometimes, especially in the afternoon, time drags. However it soon passed and another day at work came to a close. I have to work 7am to 2pm tomorrow!

At night Tufty Club wasn't as bad as usual but still pot. Me and Bes talked to some wenches all night and I'm getting to know one of 'em, she's a belter.

Saw Paul and Sayes and apparently they're going to North Wales for a holiday together, dirty dog!"

July 7th, Tuesday... "Stupid me got up at 5.45am and went to work. Working with Dave Challander isn't too bad but he is too oldish and mature to really talk to much, not about things we both like anyway. It dragged on in the morning, dead slow but by dinner-time I could look forward to going home.

When I got off the bus in Wigan I met Bes and we went shopping. I bought a pair of 'Huskie' jeans in the sale. Bes got a Ben Sherman shirt from CD. At night me, Bes and Mog went around town but there wasn't much to do, never is here."

'Bes' and I had known each other throughout the previous five years at school and as fellow Latics fans, though he wasn't as obsessed as Paul and I. He was quite tall and gangly, with dark wavy hair. Never academically gifted, Bes suffered at the hands of teachers who struggled to control his cheekiness and 'couldn't care less' attitude. He often found himself facing detention or doing 'lines' as a result. But Bes was bright in other ways being very 'street-wise' and also interested in how things worked. He eventually forged a successful career as an electrician.

Bes had a wicked sense of humour, always quick with a retort and confident enough to approach any girl he fancied though equally able to play the winsome, shy boy if it suited his ends. He was, I suppose, the irascible rogue personified and perhaps it was this that made him attractive to the girls. His long-suffering girlfriend of 1970, Judith, once assured me that Bes had "lashes to die for." I hoped and prayed that she was referring to his eye-lashes and nothing more.

July 8th, Wednesday... "I don't like Wednesday 'cos there are still three working days left! Work wasn't bad but we seem to be doing a lot just lately, I haven't known it like this before. Never mind, holiday next week! Seems I don't get any holiday money 'cos I've only worked here three weeks. I came home and had a bath then watched golf and cricket on TV. Me, Bes and Benny mucked about at night but there isn't much to do in Wigan ever."

July 9th, Thursday... "Work was bloody awful. David was in a bad mood, dead grumpy and we were dead busy all morning too 'cos of a certain order that was really thick. The paper was more like cardboard and eventually broke the burst machine we use for testing the paper. We were so busy that we had no time even for our dinner-break, was I glad to leave that place with my pay-packet of £9 6s 1d.

Bes didn't turn up in Wigan so I went home and went to sleep! After tea I went round to Bes's house which is mad, and then we went up town. Met Paul and Sayes just back from Wales with big grins on their faces but saying nowt."

July 10th, Friday... "Beautiful morning and work was dead easy, one machine closed down at 8.30am and the rest at midday. The entire factory has closed for the summer hols so after a quick clean up of the lab we were away at 1pm great!!

Met Bes in Wigan and I bought a pair of shoes and a Levi jacket for my hols (Me and Paul leave for Bournemouth tomorrow!). I spent £6 10s 0d altogether. Played cricket outside Paul's house, his neighbours are a grumpy lot.

Tufty Club again at night, pot it were, as usual. Came

home about 12.00 and packed my suitcase then had
a bath."

July 11th, Saturday... "Dad woke me up dead early and
I went round to Paul's. We caught the coach with his dad
driving of course. Made good time and arrived in London
at tea-time. London looks great but a bit too busy for me.

Arrived in Bournemouth at 7pm and booked into our
hotel. Had a good look in town, plenty of bint around, the
only snag is how to get 'em. There is quite a nice wench
working in the hotel, there may be more but we've only
been here five minutes. Came in and watched TV then
went to bed."

July 12th, Sunday... "In the morning it was very sunny
but rather windy on the sea-front. We sunbathed for a
while and then went into the sea. It was too cold though
because of the wind. In the afternoon we had a good look
around town and onto the pier. All the locals talk funny
and most of the girls are either too old and have lads
anyway, or they're with 'mummy and daddy.'

At night we tried to find somewhere to go that
seemed decent and would serve us ale but we just
ended up farting around nowhere in particular."

July 13th, Monday... "It was scorching hot so Paul and
I went swimming in the sea and sunbathing all morning.
There was an Italian girl on the beach who was very nice
indeed. She left when we did to find something to eat.
She actually tried to speak to me but I got all flustered.
Typical me that and no danger!

We spent all afternoon on the beach again but I took
my radio this time. We both got sunburnt loads and our
legs and shoulders are bloody murder now. At night we
went to a club and got absolutely bloody piss't drunk.
I came back to the hotel room and was sick three times
in the waste bin, awful it was. Paul was OK."

July 14th, Tuesday... "It was bloody raining when we
woke up but cleared up a bit and we went into the town
centre of Bournemouth. It's a bit grand, rather posh

really. In the afternoon we caught a bus to Bournemouth's football ground which isn't bad really, not as big as Latics' of course.

We bought some magazines, 'Penthouse' and 'Mayfair', and went back to the hotel where we read them as the rain poured down outside."

(Of course such magazines were purchased purely for the interesting articles contained within; articles about motoring or music and fashion. We found the glossy photos of scantily clad ladies to be nothing but a distraction.)

"Later it cleared up so we went back down to the beach and watched a huge dredger-type boat unloading tons of sand onto the beach. Apparently the beaches down here aren't sandy enough or something daft like that. At night we had a few drinks and eyed up the local talent."

July 15th, Wednesday... "It wasn't raining when we got up for breakfast but it was rather cloudy and windy. We went into town and had a good look around but there wasn't much doing. One minute it would be hot and then cloudy but at least the rain kept off.

I bought a film for my camera and then we went into the amusement arcade and spent a load of money too.

'Fartin Around'; Bournemouth, 1970

I took some photos and we went back to the hotel.
After dinner we went for a drink in the Exeter Hotel
but everything is too dear for us. The nightclubs want
a quid just to get in!"

July 16th, Thursday... "Went into W.H. Smith's
bookshop and had a good look around but didn't buy
anything, cash is running out. We went to Papa Luigi's,
a local café, for our lunch. I bought my dad some presents.
We had a good look around the record shops and stalls.

There isn't much to do at night because all the girls
are 18 or older and the clubs cater for them only. We had
a drink or two in the Exeter then went to Papa Luigi's
again for supper then off to bed."

July 17th, Friday... "We woke up late and hurried for our
breakfast. I didn't know you were only supposed to have
juice OR cereal, I've been having both all week. Bought
a paper and read about Lancashire then went to W.H.
Smith's where I bought my mum a present.

We had our dinner in Papa Luigi's again and then
I bought a book, 'Fanny Hill' which I read while we
listened to England vs Rest of the World on the radio.
The weather was cloudy but dry so I suppose we can't
complain. Lancashire beat Middlesex at Lords, great. We
farted around at night then watched the Commonwealth
games on TV."

In the summer of 1970 there was great opposition to the South African
political regime and its racist apartheid policies. The 'Stop the Tour'
campaign proved to be successful with the South African tourists being
replaced hastily by a 'Rest of the World' team. This was my first real
inkling that sport and politics were inexorably connected. It was the
first time also that I stopped to consider what racism was all about.
England got hammered in the series 1–4. So whilst we have arguably
made major improvements in term of racism in sport, the England
cricket results have a disappointing air of familiarity.

July 18th, Saturday... "After breakfast that daft woman
asked us to go with Iris and her sister tonight. We went
on the beach and had a rest and a sleep while we

> pondered whether to go out tonight or night. It's our last
> night but we haven't much cash left.
>
> We had our dinner and decided not to go out with
> them, however... we stayed in our rooms pretending to
> be asleep but in the end we went out with them and had
> a great night. We went to a local club all night and then
> spent an hour or so in the hotel lounge before crashing to
> sleep at 3am!"

This was an important lesson hard learnt. If you go to a strange town,
and Bournemouth was very strange to us northern 'Wigginers', always
ask the locals where to go and what to do. If we hadn't been such
tongue-tied, shy morons we could have had a cracking week of sun,
sea, booze, and teenage romance. Iris and her sister were waitresses at
the Pembroke Hotel, our home for the past week. They had made it
clear from the off that they'd be only too happy to show us their town.
Another lesson learnt; as the Geordies put it, "shy bairns get nowt".

This holiday was the first either of us had ever enjoyed without
parental control. Just how we managed to waste an entire week doing
so very little is shrouded in a veil of adolescent indolence and lethargy.

> **July 19th, Sunday...** "We got up at 7.30am rough as a
> dog's arse. Caught a taxi to the coach and had a good
> trip back. We only stopped once and it was pouring
> down but there was still people swimming in the sea.
> We also stopped at Keele service station, scene of last
> season's 'boot boys' incident when we all nearly got a
> hammering!
>
> We eventually got to Wigan about 6.30pm and Paul's
> dad took me home. I returned home to an empty house,
> parents on hols. I got in and had to do a load of washing,
> I've not finished yet neither I bet. I watched telly and
> went to bed, well and truly bugger't!"

> **July 20th, Monday...** "Paul came around and we went to
> Latics' to see if they'd done owt while we were away.
> They've built a tea bar and bulldozed the Shevvy End
> ready for terracing but that's all."

Actually Wigan Athletic had undertaken considerable improvements
at Springfield Park during the close season. The pitch had been re-laid

and the Supporters' Club improved. Also a new shop and canteen had been built, plus tarmac laid on the approaches to the ground. Jack Case had even built a new training area to the rear of the Springfield end. Any Latics fans who remember Springfield Park as a decrepit wreck of a stadium at the end of its life should remember just how much money, relative to income, was spent on improving it and then keeping it up to standard.

> In my opinion football grounds should be curved in design, they should be noisy, intimidating and atmospheric, everything that the DW is currently often not

We were very proud of our stadium, the biggest in non-league football and, at that time at least, constantly being improved. This all meant that we were growing with the club. We felt part of it; I actually helped to build parts of the stadium! My personal contribution to the construction of the terracing is out with the time period of this diary but if you ever noticed a crush-barrier behind the goals at the Springfield end out of alignment, it was partly my fault, allegedly.

Springfield Park certainly wasn't an instant, made-to-measure, state-of-the art stadium like the current set-up but personally I don't particularly like the DW Stadium. There, I've been and gone and said it. In my opinion football grounds should be curved in design, they should be noisy, intimidating and atmospheric, everything that the DW is currently often not. It is of interest to note in Gordon Milne's interview that he and the players experienced the lack of atmosphere at Springfield Park whilst we, the fans, felt quite the reverse.

Back in 1970 the modest ground improvements that were undertaken gave great cause for excitement as the new season approached. It went some way to compensate for the fact that my hero, Tony McLoughlin, had been sold. Even in those days I was baffled by management decisions. That managers, football or otherwise, should make decisions I disagreed with, was to be a major problem in my life. This was to be particularly problematical in my career, understandably ruining any aspirations to management I may have had, but someone has to be the voice of reason eh?

> "It's only two weeks till we play St. Mirren in a friendly, can't wait. I stayed in this afternoon and listened to the test match on TV. Then I had a bath. Me and Paul had a few drinks then went to Tufty Club. We had a laugh but I wish I was courting."

July 21st, Tuesday... "I went round to Paul's in the morning and we played cricket in the rain before I went home for my dinner. I had mushrooms and baked beans if you please! There's still no picture on the telly, so I rang the TV repair man who'll come as soon as possible, he said. He'll probably come next week with my luck. I listened to the Test Match on the radio and just mucked about all afternoon. Lancs lost, terrible.

Paul said he'd come round but didn't, so I went into town anyway. Nowt doing so I came home and listened to the radio. A chap from Dad's office phoned me to say Dad had been promoted so I phoned to tell him."

When I left a message at the holiday park reception for my dad to phone home I'm sure he thought I'd burnt the house down or been arrested. He took the news of his promotion with surprising calm. Of course he knew something about this promotion that I didn't, more of which later...

July 22nd, Wednesday... "I had to stay in all day waiting for the TV man to come, he never arrived. Paul came round in the afternoon and we played cricket in the garden and listened to Lancs vs Somerset on the radio. Lancs won by four wickets, they're a great team this year and could win the treble."

This was a 'golden era' for Lancashire Cricket Club, with players like Farokh Engineer, Clive Lloyd, Harry Pilling, 'Flat' Jack Simmons, and Peter Lever. Lancashire played exhilarating cricket. This was particularly true in the new one-day format where they achieved a hat-trick of Gillette Cup victories and the John Player Sunday league to boot. In terms of excitement and success on the pitch, the exploits of Lancashire Cricket Club were a direct substitute for the 'buzz' of Wigan Athletic and football in general during the close season.

"I had a bath and then made my tea. I also did some baking, an apple pie I made and it was great too. All my

mates and their girlfriends all came round at night. They
all went upstairs snoggin' all 'cept me, like usual."

July 23rd, Thursday... "Bes slept in my room last night.
We got up and went for a paper and some food and
I cooked us breakfast. Went to Paul's and we went into
town to pick up Paul's record player. Still not ready, we
are lost without it.

Bes and I cooked a great dinner of chips, beans and
eggs; tasted lovely. Judith came in the afternoon and she
and Bes had their usual fight and break up, only to make
up again.

Paul and Sayes stayed in our house for the evening
while me and Bes went to Latics' Club where there
wasn't much doing. I am running very short of cash
now, too short, never mind, my parents are home on
Saturday."

July 24th, Friday... "The stupid optician phoned at
9.30am and woke me up. Stayed in all morning then went
for a pie for my dinner but they had none left so I got a
tin of beans instead. I went to Paul's in the afternoon and
Dave came round too. He soon left and we played cricket
in the street.

I went home and got ready for piggin' Beachcomber.
Dead chep it was again but some quite nice girls in on
Fridays. Stew Fenton and I walked up home. I met Sue
Carrington on the way, she is very nice now!"

July 25th, Saturday... "I woke up and got my breakfast
and then went to Paul's. We went into town and I picked
up a joint from Wayne and bought a pie for my dinner."

(I feel obliged to point out that on this occasion 'a joint' was actually
a joint of meat. Wayne was my brother-in-law who worked at Frank
King's butchers in the market.)

"After dinner Paul came round and we played cricket
in the garden but it got too windy. Mum, Dad and the
kids got back about 6.30pm and Dad gave me 30s to
cover the service charge at the hotel."

"At night me and Paul went to Tufty Club again, as usual it was rank, awful. However Judith is very nice but Bes and her really like each other."

"Daft news today... Dad's promotion apparently means we have to move to South Shields by Christmas!"

July 26th, Sunday... "What a bastard's trick, eh? Dad's promotion means we have to move to South Shields. Today it poured with rain, I can understand why.

I don't want to leave Wigan, not with Latics, friends, job and everything I know here but I can't leave my family either. It's bloody rotten but I will have to go to South Shields with them. This is what Dad has worked hard for, for ages. I can't reward him by throwing it back in his face just 'cos I don't like where he has been posted. Still, it might be better than Wigan I suppose but I doubt it.

Me and Paul went in the park but nowt doing so I came home. I went to Latics at night then watched TV."

(I was to get a less than alluring insight into life in South Shields when Latics drew them away in the FA cup, more of which in the November entry.)

July 27th, Monday... "It started to rain as I got off the bus and didn't stop all day or night except for small intervals. Back to work again today and it was great. A new lad started so I had to help him out and that. He's a nice lad but a bit too cocky. We didn't do much at work because one of the machines is closed down and we were over staffed anyway.

> Dad's promotion means we have to move to South Shields. Today it poured with rain, I can understand why

When I got home I'd got a letter asking me to go for trials at Latics. You just never know, Paul might be watching me play soon, some hope! At night Judith finished with Bes, but didn't! I had a word, she cried, now they're friends again now."

July 28th, Tuesday... "Went to work like usual, Bournemouth seems like ages ago. Hard work today too.

A new lad has started which meant I had to help Dave
Lord with the effluent inflow and outflow recording,
every two hours too! Passed the time anyway. I got
soaked yet again on the way home, wish I could get
my motorbike right now.

Thinking about Bes and Judith's row last night,
it all ended in tears. I did feel sorry for her; she's learnt
her lesson this time anyway. Why am I always helping
my pals out with their wenches when I've no wench of
my own?

Went to Paul's to phone for my CSE results but
they haven't arrived at Korky's yet. We talked about
tomorrow's trial at Latics and then I went home."

July 29th, Wednesday... "Went to work at Cooke &
Nuttall's as usual but had to work in the Control Lab.
I spent all day on the burst machine, testing paper.
The stupid machine burst, spilling oil all over me and
my shoes.

I nipped home at 5pm and went to Paul's. Had my tea
then went to Latics for a trial. I didn't get enough of the
ball really, doubt they'll sign me, but the word is that
they have signed Derek Temple, seems a fair choice I
suppose. I walked up home with Andrea, who is very
nice indeed now."

July 30th, Thursday... "Stupid idea this working
business. A firm has sent back an order complaining that
it wasn't up to spec. This meant I have had to burst-test
every single sample, all on my own too and there have
been 350 samples returned. With ten bursts on each one
that is 3,500 bursts I've done and still more to come! Well
I did that all day which was boring but time passed
quickly enough.

At 5.30pm I went into Horwich, had a bite to eat and
went to cricket practice with the lads from work. It was
a good laugh and I should hold my place in their team
I reckon.

I've finally got my CSE results; two grade 1 passes,
two at grade 2, two at grade 4 and one grade 3. Not bad
for me, Dad is going to give me £3 for the results."

July 31st, Friday... "Went to work again and finally finished off all those burst tests. The end of which proved we had got the spec right in the first place! I did nothing in the afternoon which is very nice indeed. I didn't do very much all day actually which is a rather pleasant arrangement.

I am dying to see what Derek Temple is like. At £2,000 I hope he is a belter and waltzes round all the NPL defences!

At night I went to FAG *(Folk and Arts Group)* and it's great stuff. Later me and Paul saw the Ras boys give a lad a right kicking, blood in the gutters and everywhere. This reminded us to stay pally with them!"

So July saw a mid-summer holiday flash by in a blur of alcohol excess and sexual frustration.

Lancashire Cricket Club temporarily filled the gap created by the football close season. But will employment give meaning and satisfaction to our diarist's life? Well, what do you think?

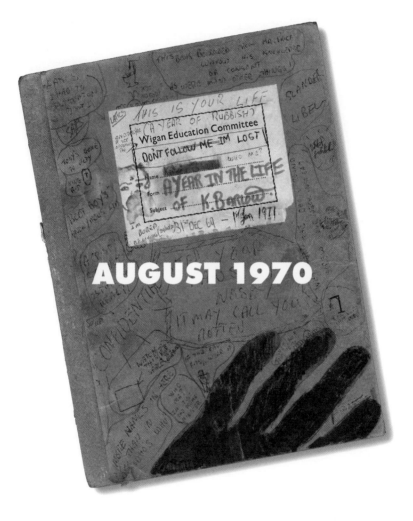

AUGUST 1970

In which, greasers, ghosts and Jehovah's Witnesses seek to distract me from the football pre-season build up.

August 1st, Saturday... "I got up and went round to Paul's. On the way I saw Andrea working in the dry-cleaners and stopped to have a word with her. I do think she is really nice now and if she finishes with her lad I'll ask her and quick!

Me and Paul went into town where I bought our Mark a birthday present and myself a magazine. Then I went home for dinner before work. Tony was on shift at work and he's as daft as a brush but good for a laugh. Dave is good to work with, you can talk to him and he'll listen.

After work I met Paul in town and we talked until 11.45pm. Me dad went mad at me, old fashioned ****!"

August 2nd, Sunday... "I got up about 11 o'clock and just mucked about till dinner 'cos there's nowt to do on Sundays anyway. I went to work in the afternoon. Well it's great at work and I get paid for it too so I'm not one to argue.

Mum, Dad and the kids went to Garstang to see Auntie Pat and Uncle Doug, so I had to get me own supper when I got in. Oh, I remember what I did this morning, I had a bath. I knew I did something.

> These 'greasers' were leather clad, pseudo Hell's Angels without motorbikes. They went on to cause mayhem for a short time in Wigan

Tufty Club wasn't bad. A load of greasers came and blocked the doors, we couldn't get out! I went with Pat Waters after and she's a nice girl too, I'd go with her again anyway!"

These 'greasers' were leather clad, pseudo Hell's Angels without motorbikes. They went on to cause mayhem for a short time in Wigan. One of these gangs chased a teenage girl through town. In her efforts to evade their attentions she clambered onto the roof of Makinson's Arcade, fell through and cut herself badly on the glass. We saw such incidents as evidence of exciting times. I suspect that that particular girl thought otherwise.

August 3rd, Monday... "Took my pants to the cleaners, Andrea's of course! She has finished with her lad; I'll ask when I'm not on a 2pm-10pm shift. I met Paul in town and took Mick Worthington's books back and I also took a film to Boots. I tried to get Dad a map of Tyneside but they had none.

I had my dinner then went to work, caught the bus as usual, from outside Wigan Casino. It's great working with this shift, they're really good to work with.

Met Paul and Mog on the way home, Latics have beat Stirling Albion 5–2! Superb display apparently. Bobby Todd, Geoff Davies and Derek Temple all made their debuts."

August 4th, Tuesday... "I got up and went round to Paul's. On the way I stopped to see Andrea again, very nice too! Paul wasn't in so I just bought a paper and went home to watch the test match on telly.

Work was pretty easy but they do make me sweat for me money! They're good to work with and never really get annoyed with me.

On the way home Paul met me coming up Mesnes Road so we stopped and had a good chat then went home. I don't know whether to live with our Janet and Wayne instead of moving to South Shields. Perhaps I could stop there until I finish at Tech in four years time? If I can have a motorbike to get to work, then OK."

FAG was the 'Folk and Arts Group,' held in the Park Hotel. This was one of the few venues in Wigan at the time for live music

August 5th, Wednesday... "I went to Paul's in the morning and we were talking when Wep came round. All three of us went into town and Wep bought 'Groovy Girl' in Dawes' record shop. I went home and made my butties then went to work.

I'll never get as good a job as this anywhere, I know that. They're good workmates, it's easy work and great pay, what more could I ask for? Paul phoned me at work at 9.45pm and told me Latics had won 3–1 against Bradford City, great, superb, even if it's just a friendly."

(Pre-season friendly. Scorers; Milne, Fleming, and Temple. Att: 2,718.)

Sue (Sayes)

"I came home from work in time to watch Man Utd beat Hull City 5–4 on penalties in the Watney Cup."

August 6th, Thursday... "Got my photos from Bournemouth back from Boots, not bad seeing as I took 'em. Work wasn't bad, lovely pay day! I got £9 16s 6d but I actually earned £11 17s 6d, ridiculous that is. Apparently though, I get all the tax back soon, mad idea that.

Trouble with this job is I'm missing all of Latics games. They beat Bradford City 3–1 last night and Paul reckons Temple is a blinder, worth every penny. Very good, keep it up lads, at least until I can get to see some of it. I came home and watched 'Invaders' on TV."

August 7th, Friday... "Me and Paul had a kick-about in the street before I went to work. A pleasant surprise awaited me when I arrived; we were all shut down so I was allowed home, with pay! I went to FAG again."

FAG was the 'Folk and Arts Group,' held in the Park Hotel. This was one of the few venues in Wigan at the time for live music, particularly blues and rock. With drink, dope, smart girls, friendly people, and good music, what more could a 16 year-old want? The landlady was Mrs Brown, always firm but fair. If we behaved she would tolerate us, if not we were out!

Rumour had it at the time that she used to be a chorus girl in Paris, something that always fascinated me. How on earth did she end up running a pub in Wigan, I wondered?

"It was packed. I could hardly move but gradually made my way round to Paul, Sayes, and Stuart Fenton. We talked, smoked, and listened to the band, 'Fat Rats,' excellent they were too. Susan Carrington asked Paul if I wanted to go with Andrea, of course I do but Paul kept quiet, good lad."

August 8th, Sat... "Me and Paul went into town. I bought a pair of trousers from C & A's, very nice too. We got the bus up to Sayes's house but she was still in bed! So we went on to Derek's. He wouldn't come to Latics so I've resigned from him!

I had my dinner in town then went to the match. Latics were great, we beat Southport 2–0, 3,821 on, not a bad attendance for a friendly. Southport were dead dirty and we nearly bounced a load of their fans with Jack Gregory, Johnny Ras, and all them lot." *(Pre-season friendly. Scorers: Fleming and Davies.)*

"Tufty Club at night was chep again but there was a great group on. I came in at 10.30pm and just watched TV."

August 9th, Sunday... "I just farted around all morning today. Why are Sundays so boring? All the family got up late so we had a brunch and by mid afternoon I was starving. I bought some toffee and watched Derby vs Man Utd on TV, Derby won 4–1 and United were thrashed.

At night I met Bes in the Brickies, we had a great time. I mixed a pint of Guinness with pale ale and a whisky. Bes got piss't and threw up all over the place. Me and Mog were dead shamed, we all got thrown out. Went to Beachcomber, it were pot as usual, met up with Bes later and he was spewin' again!"

Why did we keep going to the Beachcomber/Tufty Club? Familiarity I suppose, because there were alternative venues. Wigan Rugby Supporters' Club, although popular with the girls, was a definite non-starter for us Latics fans for obvious reasons, wishing to keep our heads on our shoulders being one of them. We could have tried the 'Pink Elephant Club' at Aspull. It was 5s to get in but only half that for ladies. Changed days indeed, the club may well have been accused of discriminatory practice in these more politically correct days.

August 10th, Monday... "I mucked about all morning 'cos I got up late. All the family went to our Janet's new house in Leyland. For some reason we went in Danny's van. It's a nice bungalow they've got, all new things too. But it's a long way to travel to work if I move in with them. Peppy, their dog, is like our dog, Topsy, and loves to play football. He wore me out he did!

> We could have tried the 'Pink Elephant Club' at Aspull. It was 5s to get in but only half that for ladies

I just got back in time to get my butties and go to the Beachcomber with Paul. It was pot but I left at 9.30pm to catch the bus to work. It's rotten nights for me this week."

August 11th, Tuesday... "I got in from work absolutely knackered and just fell into bed. It's been 22 hours since I had any sleep and felt it too!

I find night shifts go very quickly. We usually have some 'Colorall' *(a highly valued customer of paper)* to do and even if not, we play cards or read books and magazines while we wait for paper to test. One of the machinists lost his shoe in the reel end, could have been his foot, bloody fool.

I woke up and went round for Paul who was out with Sayes so I waited in the house for him. We went to the park and played soccer, even Schos played too, what a daft twit he really is!"

August 12th, Wednesday... "I got up at about 5pm and had my tea. I made my butties then, having nothing better to do, I went to Latics. Les Ritchie was taking part in a trial and played quite well too, he scored a very good goal. I talked to Jimmy Baker for a bit while I waited for Les.

I caught the 9.35pm bus and got to work quite early. MG1 broke down, it stopped for an hour and a half while the Found kept breaking down too. So we all had a pretty easy shift. If the lads aren't making paper, we can't test it!"

Both the afore mentioned were huge, powerful, paper-production machines. Basically, pulp was put in at one end of the process and these machines produced paper at the other. Obviously there was a bit more to it than just that but my memory fails to come up with the details. Our job in the quality-control lab was to test the paper at various points of production to ensure it was meeting the customer's specification.

August 13th, Thursday... "I got up late again and watched England struggle in the test match on TV. Paul rang up and came round later. We went to Latics' Beat Night in the Supporters' Club. It wasn't bad but not enough go.

I went into town and caught my bus to work. Kev always brings in chips for supper on a Thursday and I also got my pay, so not a bad night."

August 14th, Friday... "Night shifts. Yuk! Work is OK but they seem to expect me to be an expert at a job I've only been doing for seven weeks. Got up at 3pm when me and Paul went to book our coach tickets for Gainsborough Trinity on Saturday.

Had my tea, made my butties for work, then me and Paul bought some ale for tomorrow. We went to FAG, no Sayes this week. I wonder why? The band wur 'Zelda Plum', excellent they were too. I had to leave everyone enjoying themselves at 9.30pm to get the bus to work, great eh?"

August 15th, Saturday... "Came in from work at 8am and made my butties for the trip then went round for Paul. We were soon on the coach to Gainsborough Trinity and having a laugh with Jimmy, Don, and the rest of 'em. Although I was tired, a drink or two made everything great.

We had a few beers in Gainsborough's Supporters' Club before kick-off when a bloke noticed I still had my work paper knife on my belt. He threatened to get the police to me. Big Don and Jimmy helped sort it out. I left the knife behind the bar until after the game."

"The game was OK. We were 2–0 up but only drew 2–2 in the end with a pot referee." *(NPL. Scorers: Davy Breen and Geoff Davies.)* "I was shattered coming home on the coach but the noisy gits wouldn't let me sleep, they kept jabbing me and shouting in my ear to wake me up. I've been awake now for 30 hours as I write this. The things I do for Latics. Came home, wrote this and fell asleep on the settee."

And so began the 1970/71 football season. What else happened in football during that August? Well, Wilf McGuiness was formally appointed manager of Man Utd. Ferenc Puskas was still playing for Real Madrid and Mike Summerbee was sent off for Man City. The 'five step rule' for keepers was introduced. Everton beat Chelsea 2–1 in the Charity Shield and in a sign of things to come, Leeds United installed a 'police station' at Elland Road.

August 16th, Sunday... "I got up early to catch the 7 o'clock bus but it never came so I rang Kev up to explain and then got the next bus, arriving at about 10am. The shift finished four hours later too! So I didn't do badly really did I?

I went to the Beachcomber again at night and Pix came too so I had someone different to talk to for a change. His wench isn't pretty at first glance but there is something attractive about her and she has a very nice personality. I didn't feel too good all night so I went home and had a good night's sleep."

August 17th, Monday... "I'm writing this entry six days behind so I'm not sure what I did. However I remember the alarm didn't go off so I only got to work at ten to nine but they don't mind really 'cos they're often late too. We had it pretty easy at work with a machine shut down; it was 'just great man.'

At night Tufty Club was pot again, Linda kept asking me out but I won't go with her, she can get lost."

August 18th, Tuesday... "I actually got in to work on time today. Dave Smith said he would give me an early morning call from nights but I was up at 5.40am anyway so I took the phone off the hook so as not to wake Mum and the children.

When I got home I watched England lose the Test Match to the Rest of the World XI. They didn't do badly though really. Lancashire lost today too, still, they can afford to 'cos they've got games in hand.

At night me and Paul had a great game of football in Mesnes Park and by gum I need it, I'm not fit at all."

> At least I was in on time today! I got £9 14s and my flat rate is now £9 5s. Not bad seeing I'm only 16

August 1970 was the month when a brewer's dray-wagon overturned tipping hundred's of bottles of Guinness into Wallgate. Given the amount of time I spent aimlessly wandering around the town-centre I was unlucky, not to say annoyed, to not be present at the time.

It was also this month, when a young couple, estimated to be 14 to 16 years old, were seen by a local councillor having sex in broad daylight in Mesnes Park! I never did find out who they were but the local newspaper reported the incident as if were the end of civilisation as we know it. The problem of under-age sex is nothing new. Some things just never change. As I've always said, "Where there's a willy, there's a way."

August 19th, Wednesday... "Late for work this morning. So what! That Steve is often late and no one says owt. When I got home I was knackered so I'm afraid to say I fell asleep for a couple of hours.

At night Latics was great, won 3–0 vs Bradford Park Avenue with a hat-trick for Geoff Davies, he's great that mon." *(NPL. Att: 4,533.)* "Macclesfield won 6–0. Too much, never mind, just look at 22nd August! Oh yes and Gran Guest came for tea *(thrills!)*."

August 20th, Thursday... "Daft work again but at least I was in on time today! What is more it is pay day. I got £9 14s and my flat rate is now £9 5s. Not bad seeing I'm only 16.

I got home and wrote Helen a letter, doubt I'll ever see her again so why write? Then I had a bath and washed my hair, lovely now it is. Went Latics Club at night and it was great. I got merry and Judith came too.

She wouldn't drink much, I had to buy her a Babycham
yet it's Bes that's going with her!"

August 21st, Friday... "It knackers me having to get up
so early every day. It's not bad at work though, good job,
good lads to work with, and good pay, which is more
important.

Came in from work, washed me hair and straight out
again. 'Fanny' *(Andrea)* said she'd come to FAG but she
didn't so I got drunk instead. Best thing to do when a
wench lets you down I reckon. Oh yes... Paul reckons
he was hit by a ghost whilst having a slash in a derelict
house at bottom of Dicconson Street, how much sherry
had he drunk?"

I have absolutely no idea where poor Andrea got the nickname 'Fanny'
from. It meant nothing at the time and she hated it which was all the
more reason for us to use it of course.

August 22nd, Saturday... "Had to work a day shift, and
without any negotiation too. This meant I missed Latics
today. Off to work at 6.30am. Big Kev keeps battering
me, he's only muckin' about but it'll have to stop, he
soaked me too today. He reckons he wants to become
a copper. The way he bullies me he'd make a good pig
I reckon.

There was only me and Dave Challander on in the
afternoon. We had the football scores on the radio; Bolton
lost 0-4, as did Man Utd. Paul rang me up at work to tell
me Latics had won 7–0!!! Another hat-trick for Geoff
Davies too." *(NPL, vs Goole Town.)* "An impressive show of
Wigan's all round strength" reported the 'Wigan Observer'.

August 23rd, Sunday... "I went into town to be sure of
the time of the buses and bought some papers to read
about Latics. Came home and got my football-strip
together then set off for Horwich for the Cooke &
Nuttall's match. I met Kev in the pub and we had a
couple of drinks to settle the nerves! We lost 4–8 but
I scored TWO goals so I'm happy!

Tufty Club was pot again. Paul says he'll ask Fanny

for me when he next sees her so that's OK. Came home and watched 'Soft Machine' on TV, great they were."

August 24th, Monday... "I have to write two entries a night to catch up 'cos I missed out being on nights. Me and Paul met up with Wep and went to Millar's bike shop. The bikes are blasted dear but if I can pay on HP it shouldn't be too difficult. There is a Honda 175 I fancy.

Work was chep because I was all stiff after the match yesterday, so was Kev. It went quickly enough though really. Kev was on the phone to his wench for 45 minutes! After work I met Paul in town and he lent me his Jethro Tull album and a paper with Latics reports in."

August 25th, Tuesday... "Mum lumbered me with our Mark, so we painted my bedroom window. Then I went to work, it was alright but boring and that Steve doesn't half get on my nerves, he's so big headed!

I came home to Uggy *(Peter Lester, Gidlow school teacher)* in our house chatting to Mum and Dad. Don't know why, I didn't wait to ask, something to do with our Robert I think. Had a row with my mum about moving to South Shields but she can't understand, she's too old and away from me."

August 26th, Wednesday... "Mum took Mark out for the morning so I got a lie-in, and did so until midday too!

Man United won 2–0 last night at Burnley, first win of the season. Paul phoned to say that Latics are playing on Friday night so I'll miss that game too. It was in the 'Daily Express' and in the 'Evening Post' that Latics are going to build that new stand they've talked about for so long, great, eh?

Work was pot because I know I'll miss Latics on Friday night, stupid idea shifts anyway. I'm supposed to be meeting Andrea on Saturday. I could have had Friday off but Kev has already taken it so I can't, which is all a bit sickening."

August 27th, Thursday... "I got up about 10.30am and painted my bedroom window again, covering up our

Mark's mess. A chap came to the door flogging magazines
so I bought one to keep him happy, and a load of rubbish
it was too."

My purchase was partly due to naivety and partly because I was
flustered, keen to get this chap off the door-step. But I'd noticed the
title of the magazine, 'The Watchtower' and thought it may relate to
Bob Dylan or possibly Jimi Hendrix.

To this day Jehovah's Witnesses still refer to 27/08/1970 as "the day
we actually sold a magazine in Wigan."

"Work was chep, quite knackered I was at the end.
I met Fanny going up Mesnes Road and she's very nice,
big in places too, no danger!"

August 28th, Friday... "Walked Andrea to school on my
way to work. At work I discovered a catastrophe. I've got
to work Saturday and Sunday, night shift. I'm supposed
to be going out with Andrea!

Paul phoned to tell me that Latics had won again.
We beat Runcorn 3–1." *(NPL. Scorer: Fleming hat-trick. Att: 5,438.)*

"Yet another game I've missed because of work getting
in the way. Paul has agreed to phone
Andrea to explain about me working
Saturday and Sunday. He met her
later on and she said I'd to come and
see her tomorrow.

It was in the 'Daily
Express' and in the
'Evening Post' that
Latics are going to
build that new
stand they've talked
about for so long,
great, eh?

Dad says I have to move to South
Shields, ignorance. I have a good job,
plenty of mates, girlfriends, and of
course, Latics. Now I have to give it
all up, it just isn't fair."

August 29th, Saturday... "It's a real sickener having to
go to South Shields.

Paul and I went to see Fanny in the cleaners and I'm
going out with her tomorrow night instead.

Paul and I got a bus to watch Bolton draw with QPR
2–2. A chep game. Latics would give either team a run
for their money. We then went and got drunk at Paul's
house which meant I went to work rather happy."

August 30th, Sunday... "I got in from work knackered and desperate for bed only to find Joe, a friend of my dad's, in my bed! So I had my breakfast and when Joe got up I went to bed. Turned out he had been celebrating passing an exam and had supped too much to go home.

Got up at 4pm and watched Lancashire beat Yorkshire on TV therefore winning the 'John Player's League' for the second successive year.

I took Andrea to the ABC in Wigan to watch '2001: a Space Odyssey.' The film was hard to follow but superb in parts, I didn't really understand the end. Andrea is great when you get her alone and a good snogger too!"

August 31st, Monday... "I got up and went for Paul who had gone to Southport for the day. So I went down to Latics, watched them pulling down the old stand. They've also put tarmac around the new tea bar and programme shop. At night I went to watch Latics reserves beat Leyland Motors 2–0 then went off to pot night shift again."

So August came and went in a blur of alcohol and shift work, testing paper in a paper mill.

No boring school or irritating teachers but work had its drawbacks too. I had missed most of Latics early 1970/71 season due to shift work and although I finally had money to enjoy myself, work kept getting in the way.

As Oscar Wilde once said, ***"Work is the curse of the drinking classes."***

SEPTEMBER 1970

Thus far we have seen our young diarist gradually morph from an obnoxious, bored, spotty-faced schoolboy into an obnoxious, bored, spotty-faced working lad, and all this in just eight months.

Wigan Athletic FC, with 'Sir' Gordon Milne now firmly in charge, had started the 1970-71 Northern Premier League season in excellent form. Ground improvements were afoot and there were even plans for a futuristic new stand.

Meanwhile the art of making my wages last an entire week was proving even more elusive than keeping a girlfriend for a similar period of time.

The proposed new stand. It came to nothing, of course

September 1st, Tuesday... "When I got in from night shift I went straight to bed. I slept through until the chattering of the High School girls going past woke me up at about 4.30pm.

I went round to see Andrea but she is such an awkward bugger so I carried on round to Paul's. We played footy in the street then talked, played records and smoked before I had to go to stinky work. Never mind, a week's holiday next week!"

September 2nd, Wednesday... "Being stupid, as I am, I got up at 12 o'clock and was thoroughly knackered all afternoon. I got a letter from Andrea saying she is sorry she's so awkward but wants to settle down to schoolwork. So we'll have half-time I think."

155

"Met Paul on Queensway and went Latics. Good game, won 4–0 with a Jim Fleming hat-trick. There was 4,329 on and it poured down all day." *(Lancaster City, NPL.)*

September 3rd, Thursday... "I was rather tired having got up so early for no good reason yesterday. I didn't get up until 6.00pm! I cut out a report in the 'Mirror' about Latics. Jimmy Murphy and Bill Foulkes both said Latics was a great game. Then I had my tea.

I went round for Paul and we talked for a bit then went up to my bedroom to play records and talked even more. I'm sick about leaving Wigan and there is only Paul I can talk to really."

September 4th, Friday... "Mum and the kids were still asleep when I got in from work so I had to rouse them. Dad is on Tyneside working and looking for a house.

For a change there is a load about Latics in the 'Wigan Observer' so I read that before going to bed. Apparently hundreds of Wigan folk have been stung by wasps this week, they ain't got me, yet.

I got up at 4pm and had a sleepy bath. I went round to Paul's and we played records and talked."

(Led Zeppelin, Blood Sweat & Tears, Deep Purple, even Spooky Tooth were always good background music for teenage angst.)

"Went to FAG at night, Zelda Plum were on again and another great set too. Netherfield away tomorrow, my first away game of the season."

September 5th, Saturday... "The one morning I don't want a lie-in my mum lets me lie in! Dashed out of the house and bought a pie on the way. Met Don and his mates at 12.00 and we all set off to Netherfield. I never knew it was in the Lake District. I must have been asleep last time we went.

Won 2–1. Not a bad game but a draw would have been a fair result really." *(NPL. Scorers: Derek Temple and an own goal.)*

"Lancashire beat Sussex in the Gillette Cup. Went to Rave Cave again at night but as usual it were pot so

I came home and watched Liverpool 1–1 Man Utd on TV followed by Deep Purple."

September 6th, Sunday... *(Very bad writing)* "Now what did I do today? Uhmm? Oh yeh I know, I mucked about at home all morning and after dinner I went round to Paul's. Listened to Edgar Broughton Band on the radio then we played footy in the street, grumpy neighbour tried to move us on, but we didn't, did we hell!

At night I met Bes at Queensway and first we went to the Market Hotel, then the Swan & Railway, then on to the Bier Keller. Went to Tufty Club, then back to Bier Keller again. Helped Blue Rust, the live group, pack up their gear, I am a roadie!! Came home rather drunk."

September 7th, Monday... "No work this week, great! Bought a Deep Purple LP in town, 'Deep Purple In Rock'. Then I put £5 in the bank and booked the coach for Bradford Park Avenue tonight.

Me, Paul, Bes, Evvy, Barney, Joe and Soapy all made a trip back to Gidlow School but Jack Sharrock said there was too many of us to visit. Nice welcome back that eh?

Bradford away at night, their fans tried to snatch us but they only lobbed bricks at the coach. In the ground it was a bit hotter! Paul snatched a lad what called Chelsea! Stood our ground, never ran. We murdered the Yorkshire gits then they equalised in the 89th minute, bastards." *(NPL, 1–1. Scorer: Geoff Davies.)*

In truth most of the 'aggro' on the terraces involving Wigan Athletic fans was, as elsewhere in non-league football, threatened, rather than actual violence. Posturing, chanting and hurling abuse were commonplace. Usually we outnumbered the opposition and certainly had greater numbers of hard core fans willing to get involved in fighting, particularly at home games. The real test came

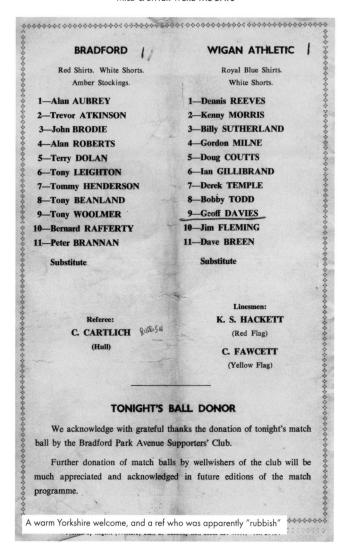

BRADFORD	WIGAN ATHLETIC
Red Shirts. White Shorts.	Royal Blue Shirts.
Amber Stockings.	White Shorts.
1—Alan AUBREY	1—Dennis REEVES
2—Trevor ATKINSON	2—Kenny MORRIS
3—John BRODIE	3—Billy SUTHERLAND
4—Alan ROBERTS	4—Gordon MILNE
5—Terry DOLAN	5—Doug COUTTS
6—Tony LEIGHTON	6—Ian GILLIBRAND
7—Tommy HENDERSON	7—Derek TEMPLE
8—Tony BEANLAND	8—Bobby TODD
9—Tony WOOLMER	9—Geoff DAVIES
10—Bernard RAFFERTY	10—Jim FLEMING
11—Peter BRANNAN	11—Dave BREEN
Substitute	Substitute

Linesmen:

K. S. HACKETT

(Red Flag)

Referee:

C. CARTLICH

(Hull)

C. FAWCETT

(Yellow Flag)

TONIGHT'S BALL DONOR

We acknowledge with grateful thanks the donation of tonight's match ball by the Bradford Park Avenue Supporters' Club.

Further donation of match balls by wellwishers of the club will be much appreciated and acknowledged in future editions of the match programme.

A warm Yorkshire welcome, and a ref who was apparently "rubbish"

at away grounds when our reputation went before us. Here the locals would gather mob-handed in an attempt to defend their patch and put us in our place.

Such was the case at Bradford that night. Their 'mob' gathered behind us and tried to push us down the terraces. They threw rocks and spat on our backs. The police meanwhile turned a blind eye to proceedings, as was usual. Although outnumbered we could only tolerate being goaded in this manner for so long. Eventually it was a case of slinking away in shame and ignominy or risk a beating and go for it. We 'went for it'. Fighting broke out, punches were thrown and kicks were landed. The unwritten rules in such brawls were:

1) always create a space to fall back to,
2) ensure skirmishes were short and brisk,
3) stay on your toes and avoid ending up the floor, and
4) if worst came to worst, 'knees up and guard the cobblers'.

A series of scuffles ensued for most of the Bradford match until mutual respect was earned and a tacit truce broke out. I suspect that a last minute equaliser for Bradford also helped in improving the mood of the opposition fans. This enabled us to get back to our coaches without too much more bloodshed, although we still had to endure a hail of bottles and bricks which again, the police utterly ignored.

> A series of scuffles ensued for most of the Bradford match until mutual respect was earned and a tacit truce broke out

The above is an accurate and fairly typical description of trouble on the terraces during that period of time in non-league matches. Elsewhere in the UK football hooliganism was a much more serious problem. But we were only 'little Wiggin'.

September 8th, Tuesday... "I got up at the stupid time of 10am. Why, when I'm off work? David, my cousin from London, came to stay with a French exchange student called Didi. He is quite pleasant but can hardly speak a word of English and I can't speak much French.

Bes and Blunt came at 1pm and we went to Wigan Tech with Paul and Les so they could register for next year. It took them ages it did. Then we went to meet Sayes and Judith from the High School.

At night Paul and I took 'Frenchy' to see Latics youth team win 3–2. I sent Andrea a nice letter too!"

September 9th, Wednesday... "I got up at 11.15am and played records and generally just mucked about until dinner-time. David, Bes, Didi and I all went to Blackpool for the day. It was dead windy and sometimes raining too. We went on the pleasure beach and an old chap gave us some free passes for most of the rides, dead lucky us eh?"

> "We looked around the shops and I bought a smart
> pendant. Then we had a pint in a pub. Got home in time
> to watch a bit of footy on telly and went to bed. A good
> day today."

We were taught French at school by a popular, if strict, teacher called
Ernie Piggot. Ernie had quite a strong 'Wiggin' accent and apparently
had learnt his French serving in France during his army days. We spent
two years of oral French/Wiggin lessons under Ernie's unique tutelage.
When our school finally went high-tech through the use of audio
cassettes we barely recognised a French word being spoken.

Certainly my French visitor, Didi, had
trouble in making out any of our feeble
attempts at French. My cousin David, with an
A level in French, was ostensibly able to
translate. Sadly however, coming from down
south, he had problems understanding the
Wigan accent!

> "Well it's still pot,"
> said Bes. We strung
> David along for
> quite some time
> before explaining
> what 'pot' meant in
> Wigan

One example of this was when David gave
Bes and me a French 'Disque Bleu' cigarette
and asked us what we thought of the unique taste and aroma? Bes
replied, "It's pot." With great consternation David assured us it was
indeed not!

Heaven forbid that we would return home telling our parents that
'my perfect cousin' David, Cambridge Blue, friend of athlete David
Bedford and all round paragon of everything my family wished me
to aspire to, was dishing out illegal substances at Blackpool Pleasure
Beach? "No! No! No!" he implored, "it's just the way the French treat
the tobacco." "Well it's still pot," said Bes. We strung David along for
quite some time before explaining what 'pot' meant in Wigan.

> **September 10th, Thursday...** "I got up at 10.30am and
> it was pouring down, really hard too. Stupid me went to
> the library in the pouring rain. Still, I did get something
> to read.
>
> Bes came at 1pm and we went to Paul's where we
> played records before going to the High School where
> we met Sayes, Judith, and Janet Senior and walked them
> into town.
>
> Latics Club at night was great. I got a bit merry and
> now I'm very tired as I write this."

September 11th, Friday... "Stupid me got up at 9.15am I've no idea why but I did. I read the papers or a library book but decided I'd better mow the lawn before my dad came back from Tyneside. David and Didi left today too.

Bes came round and we went round to his house but it pissed down so we just stayed in playing records.

Went to FAG at night but Sayes stayed in so Paul was rather mad at her and I don't blame him. Latics vs Chorley tomorrow."

September 12th, Saturday... "I was woken by Mark, no doubt sent up by Mum. I went round for Paul at 10.30am. We went into town and I bought 'Sympathy' by Rare Bird for 4s. Great lyrics this song has.

Latics was chep, big Doug Coutts scored the winner in the 88th minute, a great header but the game was rubbish. 4,300 on, so not bad really." *(NPL Cup. First round.)*

"Paul and I got merry but not too much 'cos Paul had a flaming row with Sayes again. She will only come out when and where she wants to, so I don't blame Paul for being angry.

I got a battering in town off some lad tonight. I don't know why, I don't even know who he is. I got a good few in of my own though so hopefully he'll not be back for more."

September 13th, Sunday... "My head was still sore after last night but at least I'm not dizzy or blacking out. I went round for Paul. Guess what? It poured down all day yet again. We watched football on TV but it wasn't much good, in fact it was utter rubbish.

At night Paul went to Sayes house and Bes went to roadie with that band, 'Blue Rust'. So I decided to go to the pictures. A sex film was on. It wasn't bad but not really great. I've only just watched it and I can't even remember what it was called!"

September 14th, Monday... "Got up at 6am and dashed out to catch the bus back to work. When I got there I was the first one in the lab! The machines hadn't started and when they did they were just making mill wrappers till about 10am. So all in all we had quite an easy time of it.

After work I met Paul at Tech and we went and booked for the Lancaster game, well I did. We mucked about in Wigan at night but nothing doing so I went in and watched TV."

September 15th, Tuesday... "5.45am I got up! Stupid idea shift work. Steve didn't come in until 7.30 but I had nothing to test so we were all right. Kev was at Tech today so we were quite rushed, well I was. He's dead lazy that Steve, clever but I have to do all the donkey work for him. I went home rather tired and bought a 'Post' on the way, I called in to Paul's for a talk, mainly about leaving Wigan.

At night we went to Latics reserves who lost 1–4 but it's a ridiculous score-line, they scored three goals in ten minutes. Lancaster away tomorrow."

September 16th, Wednesday... "First one in work again today. If they're not in, I'm not testing owt, so it's cheddar. I had no money at all, no fags, no papers, nowt, I'm absolutely skint, still.

Got home about 3pm and had my tea then caught the coach to Lancaster. Chep, rotten game ended 0-0, pot it were." *(NPL.Att:1,200.)*

September 17th, Thursday... "Up at 5.45am again, dumb idea this work thing. Steve was at Tech *(hooray),* so Kev and I did the work. Pretty easy I suppose. I had another rotten dinner in the canteen then went home.

Met Paul at tea-time, him and Sayes have had yet another argument.

Went Latics club at night, not bad but not enough go. Someone broke a towel rail in the bogs and they tried to blame me! Big Don, my mate, he was bouncer too, asked if it was me! Like I'd damage Latics Club? Some lad admitted it in the end though."

September 18th, Friday... "I only got up at 8am today 'cos it's a Tech day. Alan never showed up but I found the room myself OK. We mucked about melting glass all morning. I only wish I got paid for going full-time, some bonny wenches go, not half! We did maths and physics all afternoon which I hate. At last we were allowed home.

Went to FAG again at night, Sayes was 30 minutes late, as usual. Not bad, better than the Tufty Club anyway. Sad, sad news that Jimi Hendrix was dead! But is it true???"

It was very rare for the outside world to impact upon our scribe's insular life of Latics, work, booze, pals and girls but this was one exception. Just as people can recall exactly where they were when they learnt of J. F. Kennedy's assassination, the Moon landing or even Danny Molyneux buying a round, so it was that I could recall confirmation of Jimi Hendrix's death. The great man apparently choked on his own vomit following an alcohol and drugs binge. I learned of this as I stood outside what was at the time 'Grundy's' newsagents on Mesnes Road, (opposite the Brocket Hotel in Wigan). Well we all had to be somewhere I suppose. I'd heard rumours of Jimi's death on the radio but it took that quality newspaper *'The Lancashire Evening Post & Chronicle'* to confirm any hopeful, lingering doubts.

> Just as people can recall exactly where they were when they learnt of J. F. Kennedy's assassination, the Moon landing or even Danny Molyneux buying a round, so it was that I could recall confirmation of Jimi Hendrix's death

I also recall my parents' response when I told them the tragic news. Mum said, "Who?" and Dad said, "Electrocuted himself did he? That's what you get for playing an electric guitar with your teeth." His response was equally unsympathetic when I explained the circumstances of Jimi's sad demise. "Let that be a lesson to you young man." Just what my father thought I was getting up to I dread to think. O that I were to die a rock star's death! The closest I came was when I tried to tie-dye my grandad shirt, it emerged more died than dyed.

September 19th, Saturday... "I am stupid getting up at 5.45am again and off to rotten work. It was alright but a bit boring. Kev is an absolute nutter, but time passed OK. We tried to mend my radio to get the footy scores but no joy.

We had to spend the entire afternoon with no sport, disgusting."

"I bought a 'Football Pink' in town and Latics had won 5–2! Great win that, Geoff Davies with yet another hat-trick!" *(Bangor City away, NPL. Jim Fleming bagged the other two goals.)*

"Went to Monaco at night, not bad but a bit dear and too big for my liking I think."

Manchester City announced an annual profit of £37,000, yes that's £37k, the amount that most modern Premier League players 'earn' per week!

We could have gone to the Pink Elephant Club at Aspull where Colonel Bagshot's Incredible Bucket Band appeared. They were a more than useful outfit and very popular in Lancashire at the time, but Aspull? Be fair! It was far too close to Bolton for our liking.

Alternatively, we could have enjoyed a Hot Pot Supper at the White Lion in Up Holland or even The Spinners at the Queens Hall. Only marginally less attractive than either of these mind-blowing events in Wigan, September, 1970 was 'Carry On up the Jungle' at the cinema. Little wonder we ended up in the pubs!

September 20th, Sunday... "Slept in until about 12.00 then went and bought a paper to read all about Jimi Hendrix dying. I don't like Sundays at all. Went into Mesnes Park, drank some cider, and stayed in all night. Jan and Wayne are staying until Wednesday, don't know why."

September 21st, Monday... "I got up at 9.30am and went to the library to change my books, obviously!

Stupid work again, still it could be worse, not bad really. The time went slowly though as it always does but 10pm came soon enough. Met Denise Mitchell in town, she's reet fit her and no mistake.

I went to Paul's on the way home and him and Sayes have finished, shock result that! He'd bought me a 'Post' so I could read about Latics. I told him about Kev Farrell and them lot going to Latics Club next Thursday."

It was at this point in Wigan's history that the first rumours appeared regarding the future of the Market Hall. The local press reported plans for a £450,000 re-development, the monstrosity that eventually became, in my humble opinion, a 'carbuncle' that Prince Charles ought to have objected to, namely the Galleries Shopping Centre.

Also in the local press this week in 1970 was something that I suspect would not be tolerated in more modern times. A Wigan driver was let off a driving ban despite failing the breathalyser. He successfully blamed a home-made cough remedy. Aye right!

> **September 22nd, Tuesday...** "I only got up at 12am and then made my butties for work then had my dinner.
>
> At work Kev wasn't in 'cos he goes to Tech on Tuesdays so I had to put with moaning Steve all rotten day. He gets on my nerves, lazy swine. When we get a sample he just throws it toward me, doesn't even speak my name, then walks out for another chat and a fag with his pals.
>
> Latics were playing tonight too and I missed it 'cos of work again. We drew 1–1 at Chorley, good result that really." *(NPL. Scorer: Geoff Davies.)* "Paul reckons there was loads of bovver too and I missed it all!"

Elsewhere in football in September 1970, Manchester City announced an annual profit of £37,000, yes that's £37k, the amount that most modern Premier League players 'earn' per week!

Celtic scored nine against a Finnish outfit and Everton put six past an Icelandic team. Borussia Moenchengladbach won a Cup Winners' Cup tie 16–0 on aggregate!

Man United's miserable start to the season continued with a 0-4 stuffing at Ipswich.

Ron 'the Tank' Atkinson scored for Oxford Utd as they beat Bolton. Whilst Alan Hudson scored 'the goal that never was' for Chelsea. His long-range shot hit the outside stanchion of the net and the referee, Roy Capey, gave a goal.

So whilst the days of walkovers in the early stages of European competitions may have now long gone, except for Welsh teams perhaps, it remains perversely satisfying to know that incompetent refereeing has a long and ignoble history.

> **September 23rd, Wednesday...** "Slept in until 12 noon again, great idea this! I made my butties and bought a can of soup for supper at work on the way down for the bus. I'm glad Kev was in today. It's rotten with Steven, he's so boring and always moaning, moaning, moaning."

"Work seemed to go dead quick today, probably because we had a straight run through all day, no problems. We made a new football too at last, made out of the foam from an old chair. Office footy helps pass the boring bits of the shift.

Came home and watched Arsenal beat Lazio 2–0 on TV, not bad."

September 24th, Thursday... "Up early this morning, 10.45am I made my butties and had a kip until Mum and Mark came home at noon.

Work was great! No Steve today that's probably why. Plus it is pay day. I got £12 today, not bad really. Work flew past till Paul phoned at 9pm to say that Latics vs Spartak FC is now in the balance!

I got in and had a bath. Tech tomorrow, I don't like Maths at all!"

September 25th, Friday... "Went for Paul at half-eight and went to Tech. It passes dead quickly some days. We mixed solutions, filtered them and dried them off in an oven. All very interesting but I don't know why we are doing it. We wrote a lot of notes too, time passed. From 4.30 until 6.30pm it should have been General Studies but the lecturer never turned up so we all went at 5pm.

Paul and I took advantage and went straight on a pub crawl then crawled into FAG. We both talked to Sayes, I'm sure she still wants to go with Paul."

September 26th, Saturday... "Went with Dad to buy me a motorbike off some bloke but the twit had sold it, just my luck. Dad dropped me off and I bought Deep Purple's 'Black Night' and Black Sabbath's 'Paranoid' singles in town on the way back.

Latics was chep, they didn't play well at all and only equalized late on." *(South Liverpool, at home, NPL. 1–1. Scorer: Derek Temple. Att: 3,891.)*

Paul and I went to Monaco at night again. Sayes is mad, she said she wants to go with Paul but won't because she says they are both "too young." Stupid that is.

Judith asked me so I went with her, and she is very nice

too! Hope her and Bes really have finished like she says."

September 27th, Sunday... "I got up at 11 o'clock and had my breakfast and read the Sunday papers. Then I copied up my notes from Tech until dinner-time. I woke Bes out of bed, he says he and Judith have definitely finished, and all that stuff, so "keep right on with Judith" he says.

> Paul came round and we played records and talked mainly about how daft girls are.
> I went to work on night shift and worried myself sick about Judith

Paul and I went for a few drinks and met Stew Fenton and Clarence after the Tufty Club. Janet Senior phoned our house after and I've asked her to get Judith to phone me 'cos I need a word with her."

September 28th, Monday... "I got up really quite early and went round to meet Paul in Tech. I asked Benny to lend me his boots for training on Wednesday and then I put £2 in the bank.

I came home and had a bath and let my hair dry but it still looks pot. Judith did phone after all but I still don't really know if we are going together proper or not. If not, well cheddar. Paul came round and we played records and talked mainly about how daft girls are. I went to work on night shift and worried myself sick about Judith."

September 29th, Tuesday... "I bought a paper on my way in from night shift, then had my breakfast before going to bed. Got up at 4pm and went to the paper shop. Paul said he'd come round later but he didn't so I went to see Latics training.

I met Stewart Fenton after and we went to see Bes with a message from Pat Waters. We all mucked about a bit, then Stewy and I got the bus into town where I caught my bus for work, a real waste of a day."

September 30th, Wednesday... "I got up and went for a paper. Me and Paul have decided that girls are well and truly stupid. We'll never understand them as long as we both live!"

"I went down to the Woodhouse Lane stadium for
training. Paul never went, said he was too knackered.
After training I watched Latics youth beat Barrow youth
2–1. Got a lift off Eric Ormisher to the bus stop and went
to work, it was knackering too."

Few of my contemporaries could make sense of the fluctuating moods
and demands of the girls we knew. There appeared to be no consis-
tency to their arguments or behaviour. One day they were all over
us like gravy, "Do you really fancy me? You must come to my friend's
party with me. Come and meet my parents." The next day it was, "You're
far too serious; I'm too young to go steady. I've got my schoolwork
to think about. Where do you think you're putting that hand?" For us
novices in womanly wiles it was bewildering; their stance in most
things was as clear as concrete. Such lessons in life were hard to
accept, but having said that, a lifetime's experience has left me only a
little wiser.

So, are subtle signs of change, if not maturity, beginning to appear in
our diarist's life? Are they the green shoots of adulthood? Well hardly.

OCTOBER 1970

Recently our diarist has been gradually weaning himself off the Beachcomber Club for venues new. Whilst the girls were dancing around their handbags to Freda Payne, Desmond Dekker and Jimmy Cliff, Wigan's answer to Sir Francis Bacon was enjoying Free, Led Zeppelin, Jimi Hendrix, Ten Years After, and Jethro Tull.

Such musical tastes marked a socially important distinction at the time. Could you really go out with any girl who thought Pink Floyd and Deep Purple were the latest mascara as recommended by 'Jackie' magazine? (Well yes actually if she was pretty, easy or preferably both.)

And so it was that in October 1970, whilst BP were discovering North Sea Oil, I was discovering Tartan Bitter, Greenhall's Mild and Newcastle Brown Ale.

October 1st, Thursday... "The usual routine, in from night shift, had my breakfast whilst reading the paper and went to bed. Mum tries to keep the kids quiet but doesn't always manage it. Today I slept through until 3.30pm when I got up and went for a postal order for Mum and bought an evening paper to read about Latics.

> Went to the Market Hotel at dinner-time, got a fright when my dad spotted me in the snug. I forgot he was back from Tyneside, I near shit missel

After tea I went with Bes to Latics Club's Beat Night but not for long. Judith has asked Bes to go with her again so she can get knotted! I left Latics Club in a huff and went to Paul's. He came to work with me for my pay. We both got soaked on the way back, bloody useless Wigan buses."

October 2nd, Friday... "Went into Tech, the novelty is wearing off, it was dead chep all morning. Went to the Market Hotel at dinner-time, got a fright when my dad spotted me in the snug. I forgot he was back from Tyneside, I near shit missel' but all he did was send half a Tartan through! He hasn't mentioned it since either. This is much worse than the battering I expect at any time. So Mum, if you're reading this, please say nowt.

I didn't feel so good in the afternoon so Keith and I went to Paul's for a skive."

"We went to the Market at night, then the Bier Keller, then FAG. Sayes went to FAG and if Paul doesn't want to go back with her, I will and no danger!

I had to leave early again for work, it wur chep."

This week in 1970 the local press revealed an interesting difference of opinion behind the scenes at Wigan Athletic that could have had significant ramifications. At a board-meeting, Chairman Arthur Horrocks was duly re-elected but not without a bit of an internal kerfuffle. The outcome of which was the resignation, after only three weeks tenure, of a certain Mr Dave Whelan. Coincidentally, it was also this month in 1970 that the Bank of England, as part of the run up to decimalisation, issued a £20 banknote.

Janice Joplin died today. That's just not right, so soon after Hendrix too. She was only 27. I always thought she was older than that, she certainly looked it

Presumably Mr Whelan had difficulty at the time balancing his commitments as a board member and counting the newly issued £20 notes rolling into his supermarket business? This was of course the same Dave Whelan who was later to become the wealthy businessman and 'saviour' of Wigan Athletic. One can only guess as to what might have happened had he not resigned from the board all those years previously.

October 3rd, Saturday... "Got in from chep Cooke & Nuttall's, I hate night shift, went straight to bed. Up at 2pm and off to Latics reserves. They lost 1–3 and even the first team lost 1–2 at Boston Utd." *(NPL. Scorer: Derek Temple Att: 2,100.)*

"Me and the lads played soccer in the car park until the result came through then I went home.

Paul and I went to the Monaco at night, it was alright but that's all. Judith went with some lad but I don't care anymore, there's plenty more fish in the sea, *(there's not!)*"

October 4th, Sunday... "Lovely lie-in this morning until 12.15pm!! Great stuff.

I went to Paul's and we watched Sunderland beat Bolton 4–1, ha, ha! We also made out a fixture list, should get a team soon."

This was a cringe-worthy idea of listing all the girls we thought we had a chance with and listing dates on which either one of us would ask them out, sad or what? Needless to say it went no further than the planning stage.

"Janice Joplin died today. That's just not right, so soon after Hendrix too. She was only 27. I always thought she was older than that, she certainly looked it.

Nowt to do in Wigan on a Sunday, we went to the Bier Keller but it was empty. Went round to Stew Fenton's then went home. Pot isn't it?"

October 5th, Monday... "I got up at six in the morning and it was pitch black. Work was alright, a bit boring but that's all. Steve didn't come in thank goodness! I don't like him one bit. It goes quickly this 7–2 shift probably because it's only seven hours. I went for a 'Post' but there isn't much about Latics in it.

At night Paul and I went to see Leeds vs Wigan schoolkids at Latics. It poured down and we got soaked coming home. Paul phoned Janet Senior from the phone box but she was out."

October 6th, Tuesday... "When I got to work Steve was actually in on time! It was pretty rough really 'cos Kev was at Tech but we managed to ignore each other by staying busy. About 10 o'clock I felt quite ill but it soon passed. I came home but still felt ill. I went for a paper but there was nowt worth reading in that.

At night I went to Paul's but felt even worse. We played records but I had to come home and go to bed."

October 7th, Wednesday... "I hadn't gone to work 'cos me guts were rotten. I spent the day muckin' about playing records, reading, and shitting. Me belly gradually got better and after a bite to eat I felt fine again.

Went to see Latics play Netherfield at night, Geoff Davies scored in the first minute and Derek Temple in the second half. Only 1,600 on." *(Ashworth Trophy.)* "Judith and Sayes came to the game and we walked them into town. Judith seems to still like me so I'll ask her again soon."

October 8th, Thursday... "Well I thought I'd better go to work so I got up at 5.45am, had my breakfast and walked into town for my bus.

We had rather a busy day! Steve was at Tech, thank goodness. However the time passed quick enough.

Sayes and Judith walked down from school and Judith lent me a book, very good it is too. They're both going to Latics tomorrow so I'm going with Judith, very good too! At night me and Paul went to Latics Club. Jack, Greg, and them lot were there, loads of fighting, a bloodbath, lovely!"

October 9th, Friday... "I went for Paul at 8.30am and we went to Tech, it was freezing too. It's alright is Tech but dead boring and too much writing.

Me and Paul went to the Market Hotel again for our dinner. Colin, the landlord, serves great Lancashire cheese and onion barm-cakes. They are fantastic washed down with a pint of Tartan, superb.

At night we went to Latics, they won 4–1, great display." *(vs Morecombe, NPL. Scorers: Geoff Davies x 2, Billy Sutherland and Davy Breen. Attendance: 3,525.)*

"Sayes and Judith came to the match. Sayes finished with Paul once and for all, so they both say. Judith ignored me all night and mucked about with Janet. WENCHES ARE MAD."

October 10th, Saturday... "I got up quite early, about 9.45am and went to Paul's to tell him we were going to Rochdale with Peaky to see 'the Villa'.

We left about 11.30am and had lunch in a pub in Wigan. A clever piece of 'how's your father' on British Railways saw five of us get to Rochdale and back for 5s 9d!"

This deception involved buying one valid return ticket and a platform ticket. We hid in the toilets on the train whenever the inspector came round and then passed both tickets back and forth between the platform railings on arrival at either end.

"Very good it was too, chep game but loads of Villa fans who we joined up with, loads of shouting, great it was."

"Went Monaco at night, it was pot but still a night out. Wigan rugby have lost 23–0 to St Helens, sick on them, 23,000 on to see it too, ha, ha."

Bobby Charlton played his 500th league game today, Man Utd marked the occasion by losing 0-1 to Crystal Palace.

October 11th, Sunday... "I've amazed myself at having kept this diary up to be honest! I'm a good lad aren't I?

I got up about 11.30am and just mucked about the house, reading the paper and copying up my Tech notes. Mum, Dad and the kids all went to Jan and Wayne's but I stayed at home. Then I watched football on the telly. Luton are great this year, that young lad Malcolm MacDonald could be a belter.

I made my own tea, baked beans on toast, and then went for Paul who hadn't got back from London. I went into town and had a couple of drinks then met a lad I knew so we went to the Bier Keller and had a couple more.

> Then I watched football on the telly. Luton are great this year, that young lad Malcolm MacDonald could be a belter

I came home and ordered a radio out of the 'Daily Express' for £8 – too much!"

October 12th, Monday... "I had a lovely lie-in today until 11.30am. I had my dinner and made some bacon butties then went to rotten work. It wasn't bad really but this shift work is no life. It may bring in the money but I don't think it's really worth it.

Anyway I got a £1 per week pay rise today which means I'm now on £10 5s for a flat week, not at all bad really. I'm having Wednesday off 'cos it's due me and I may as well have it off now. I came home from work and called in on Paul on the way home."

October 13th, Tuesday... "I got up at 10 o'clock and had my breakfast before going down to the bank. I drew out £9 and had a look around Tech but nowt doing. I went to the Post Office and got £7 19s 6d of postal orders for my radio. I sent them off and then just mucked about the house until it was time for work. Work was pot because of course Kev isn't in on Tuesdays.

On the way home I met Denise Mitchell in town, she's bonny and no danger! I went up to Paul's, then came home and went to bed."

> Rugby fans all turned up but as usual they never did owt, right mardy them lot. They come on our patch shouting and threatening us then, when we rush 'em, they just run off!

October 14th, Wednesday... "Mum woke me up at 10am and made me look after our Mark while she went to the bank. I read a book till dinner and just mucked about.

I went to Tech and met Keith who was skiving like usual so we went to watch Paul and Les doing games.

Went to Latics at night, good game too, we beat Scarborough 3–1." *(NPL. Scorers: Jim Fleming x 2, (1 pen), and Bobby Todd. Attendance: 3,366.)* "Rugby fans all turned up but as usual they never did owt, right mardy them lot. They come on our patch shouting and threatening us then, when we rush 'em, they just run off!"

October 15th, Thursday... "Someone came looking round our house while I was still in bed; the fools woke me up from my lie-in."

This abrupt interruption to my siesta came as a forceful reminder that my family were actually going to move house and relocate to Tyneside. I had been hoping that if I forgot about it perhaps my parents would too, maybe the whole idea would go away? Denial was an unfamiliar concept to me at this point in life. Prospective purchasers bursting into my bedroom while I was still in bed however, abruptly disabused me of any such hopes.

"Mum and Mark came back from the shop where she works with a pie for my dinner. So I made my butties and went to work on back shift. It went quite quickly 'cos McMahon was at Tech so we were busy. Got paid! I've had a rise at work, I'm now taking home £10 5s a week. But how can I make it last? I suppose it's not bad money but shift work is no life for a young lad like me."

Jim Fleming

October 16th, Friday... "I got up at 8 o'clock and had my breakfast before going round to Paul's. We went to Tech which wasn't bad really. We do a lot of experiments and that passes the time quickly enough. We should have had General Studies at 4 o'clock but I didn't want to do it so I went home for tea. What's the point if I'm moving house anyway?

Paul and I went to FAG at night, it wasn't bad. Susan Carrington has turned bloody gorgeous suddenly, maybe a possibility?"

October 17th, Saturday... "Paul and I went into Wigan and I bought a pair of trousers and some hamster bedding. Paul bought some ham. There wasn't much doing so we went home. I watched 'On The Ball' and finished my book, 'Skinhead', great it was too.

Me and Paul went to Latics. It was a great game, we won 5–0." *(NPL, vs Gainsborough Trinity. Scorers: Geoff Davies, hat-trick, Jim Fleming and Graham Turner. Attendance: 4,236.)*

"Geoff Davies scored his 4th hat-trick of the season so far, 17 goals in 14 games! Good crowd on too, great Kop, I've lost my voice! Everyone is impressed with Latics' playing style.

Me and Paul got some sherry off Wep and celebrated in Paul's house before heading off to the Monaco, not much doing so we just came home.

Jack Charlton scored for Leeds then Bobby scored for Man Utd in the same game, odd eh?" *(Leeds Utd away. Score: 2–2.)*

October 18th, Sunday... "I cannot stand Sundays at all! There's nothing to do. I'd go to church but I don't believe in it, God yes, but church no.

I read about Latics in the Sunday paper and then had an egg for my dinner. At Paul's house we watched Man City on telly and Man United drawing at Leeds. We mucked about trying to think what to do at night but couldn't think of owt.

I came home for a bath then Paul and I wandered around town for a bit."

October 19th, Monday... "I slept in until about 11.30am. Then, after dinner, I went into town and paid the bill at the Coal Board for Mum. I met Paul at Tech and we walked up home. It poured down all afternoon, so much so that Judith wouldn't walk down for the bus, soft fool.

It was Latics vs Chorley at night. A pot game, it always is against them bums! We had a great Kop going though, especially in the second half, superb it was, dead noisy! 0-0 the score." *(Lancashire Challenge Cup. Attendance: 2,200.)*

"I caught the bus with Grenville on my way to work. Work was dead boring."

October 20th, Tuesday... "I got in from night shift very tired, had my breakfast and went straight to bed. I got up in time to meet Judith on her way down from school but again she didn't come. It was very cold waiting though! I have got another rotten boil on my lip and it is rather sore.

Geoff Davies scored his 4th hat-trick of the season so far, 17 goals in 14 games! Good crowd on too, great Kop, I've lost my voice!

Paul and I played records and that before phoning Susan Carrington and asked her to remind Judith about the book.

Work was alright, not bad, not good."

October 21st, Wednesday... "I can't find much to write about when I'm on night shift 'cos I'm in bed all day and there's nowt to do in Wigan at night. I got up at 3.30pm to meet the High School girls but Judith never showed again. I've told Susan Carrington to tell Judith I'll sell her book to a lad at work if she doesn't meet me to collect it.

Had a bath, made my butties, watched TV and went to work. Really I'm glad I have to leave this job 'cos it's pot working shifts."

October 22nd, Thursday... "Came in from work and read about European football. Then had my breakfast before getting into a cold bed.

I got up about 3.30pm. Went to the paper shop on Mesnes Road, yet again Judith didn't turn up, so as far as she's concerned I've sold that book! I bought a paper and came home."

"I went to Latics' Club at night and had a drink before Bes and I went to Horwich for my wages. We bought some chips and then went home. Talk is that the rugby fans are coming with us to get the Macc fans, great stuff!"

October 23rd, Friday... "When I got to Paul's he was still in bed so I just went on down to Tech. I felt rotten so I didn't go in to lessons. Me, Keith and Evvy went to choose our prizes for the school speech day.

In the afternoon I went up to Paul's and we played records and talked before going round for a paper.

We went to FAG at night, not bad. I asked some wenches for Paul but they wouldn't go with him. Left at 9.30pm, I had to leave to get the bus for work."

October 24th, Saturday... "I got in from night shift and went straight to bed at 8.30am. Got up again at 11.30am and went for Paul to go to Macc, away! Been looking forward to this game for weeks. We met Ewol but he couldn't take Paul, no room in his car. This meant Paul missed the coaches too, disaster for him. There was 1,500 Latics fans went and we had a great time. Reet noisy Kop going on with trouble throughout the game and after. I nearly got snatched again, all alone outside the ground, but managed to leg it. Don't know why the Macc fans keep picking on me?

> Fantastic day, now we are kings, knocked them off the top spot of NPL!!

Great game it was, fatty Fidler had 'em one up at half-time but second half it was all Latics, Jim Fleming played brill. They scored an o g and Fidler even missed a penalty, twice, near the end!" *(Won 3–1, NPL. Scorers: Geoff Davies, Jim Fleming and Sievewright og. Attendance: 4,256.)*

"Fantastic day, now we are kings, knocked them off the top spot of NPL!!

Went to Monaco by myself at night but it was quiet, I had to leave at 9pm to go to work again."

October 25th, Sunday... "I had to work until 6am but because of the buses on a Sunday I didn't get home until 9.30am, stupid."

"I stayed in bed until 5 o'clock then got up to have my tea. I felt rotten but I got some fags and went round to Paul's. Paul wasn't in a very happy mood either but we talked and smoked and then went for a walk in town. Pretty empty, like usual so we went home, I was very, very tired."

October 26th, Monday... "I had to get up early again today to go to rotten work. Work was alright but they are always calling me pot and they don't do much themselves. I do what I'm told, what more do they want? The morning shifts pass quite quickly although I usually feel really sleepy mid-morning. It's not healthy getting up at that time.

> At night I went round to Paul's but there was nowhere to go so I just came home and watched Mohammad Ali destroy Jerry Quarry in three rounds on TV

I met Paul in Lowe's Cafe before we went and booked our coach seats for Skem away tonight. As soon as we'd booked we found out Latics are sending the reserves! It was a night out I suppose. Loads of us went and saw us get beat 0-5, but the reserves tried I suppose." *(Ashworth Trophy.)*

October 27th, Tuesday... "I'm writing this on Friday 'cos I couldn't be bothered mid-week. I know I had to get up at 6 o'clock again, it's murder! I feel really bad about 10 o'clock, dead sleepy like I was on drugs.

Kev is at Tech but it wasn't too bad with Steve today really. Better than usual anyway! I went home and got a paper from the shop but not much in about Latics.

At night I went round to Paul's but there was nowhere to go so I just came home and watched Mohammad Ali destroy Jerry Quarry in three rounds on TV."

October 28th, Wednesday... "One of these days I'll catch up but I'm three days of diary writing behind. It was murder at work trying to keep my eyes open, I go all sleepy and dizzy.

After work I went to Chorley and had a great time, we won 3-2. Loads of fighting with a bunch of Chorley greasers, we had 'em! Scruffy ground, muddy, slag heap terracing and crap lights." *(Lancashire Senior Cup. Scorers: Geoff Davies and 'Sir' Gordon Milne. Attendance: 1,800.)*

October 29th, Thursday... "Now today I was really shattered at work. I've never known anything like it at all, it was a rotten feeling. It cleared up about 11 o'clock. I got paid, £14 0s 10d so that helped perk me up a bit!

I persuaded Paul to come to Latics Club at night, it was alright I suppose. Tech tomorrow, it's chep too."

October 30th, Friday... "Chep Tech today but I suppose it's better than being at work really. We did a lot of writing, taking notes, jottings, and so on. I felt rotten last lesson so I left quick.

At night I went to FAG with Paul and then on to Wigan Casino, which wasn't bad. I only got home at midnight but I did warn them."

> Great day at Alty! We bounced two of their mob and had a great Kop going, dead loud we was. We should have won but only drew 1–1

October 31st, Saturday... "After last night's over-exertions at FAG and then the Casino I enjoyed a lie-in until 10.30am.

Me and Paul went into town, I bought a Hendrix record for six bob. Great it is too, oh, and a jumper for 22s. We had our dinner in the Market Hotel, another one of Colin's cheese and onion barm-cakes and a pint. Tartan is only 1s 6d a pint there too. Then we went to Latics for the coach to Altrincham.

Great day at Alty! We bounced two of their mob and had a great Kop going, dead loud we was. We should have won but only drew 1–1." *(NPL. Scorer: Geoff Davies. Attendance: 2,865.)*

"At night I went Monaco by myself and just talked with Colin and Micky Davis all evening. Met Judith and then Sayes *(wow!)* in town on my way home."

October appears to record a subtle change in my attitudes to a number of factors. For example:

1) girls were becoming increasingly infuriating, if not positively annoying!
2) the job was losing its initial attraction,
3) the move to Tyneside was increasingly to the fore of my thinking, and finally,
4) my social life was becoming slightly more adventurous.

But it was Wigan Athletic and the terraces that continued to provide the real buzz in my life. Would I ever grow up?

Would I ever come to understand that girls were as confused about us lads as we were about them?

NOVEMBER 1970

Thus far readers may appreciate just how much colour Wigan Athletic brought to our diarist's otherwise dull existence.

With no colour TV, internet, Sky TV, CDs, texts, or mobile phones, to stay in touch with Latics, or any football club, one had to rely largely on the local print media such as the Football Pink, the Lancashire Evening Post and Chronicle or the Wigan Observer. Even then you would have to search hard to find Latics stories buried beneath the all-consuming rugby team details. As for Latics results, you would have listen to the NPL/Non-League results service tucked away on BBC Radio 4 after Alistair Cooke's 'Letter From America', (no, you young uns, not The Proclaimers.)

November 1st, Sunday... "I got up at 10.30am and went for Paul. We went to Springfield Park for some tickets for the Skem game and we had a good game of soccer in the car park while we waited with Jimmy, Dirky and them. We got our tickets easy and went home. Paul and I watched Liverpool beat Wolves on TV at his house.

I went home and had a bath, then met Bes and Judith and we went to the Bier Keller, not bad."

November 2nd, Monday... "I had a lovely lie-in for once, marvellous it was, great. I got up late and read the papers. I mucked about with nowt to do then made my tea and went to work.

> Even at 16 I had some sense of morality, you just didn't make a move on your mate's bird!

Work was alright really 'cos there was three of us for a change and it's not bad then. On the way home I called in to Paul's for half an hour then went home. I've decided that I quite fancy Sayes actually, have done for ages really."

I was understandably reluctant to make any approach to Sue (Sayes). She had been my best friend's girl for months. Even at 16 I had some sense of morality, you just didn't make a move on your mate's bird! On the other hand she was very attractive, intelligent, friendly, and seemed to quite like me. In addition I had been besotted with her, secretly, for as long as I'd known her, and now she was single. So, quite a quandary; stay loyal to my pal or follow my heart (loins)? It had to be sorted out 'man to man.'

November 3rd, Tuesday... "On back shift again but me mother woke me up at 7.30am 'cos she thought I was on early shift.

I've decided I really fancy Sayes so I've spoke to Paul and he says OK, 'cos him and her have definitely blown for full-time." (*That was it then, sorted out, 'man to man'.*)

"Paul lent me 'Deep Purple in Rock' record so I played that then waited for the Whitley High school girls to walk by. Just as Sayes and Judith came past our house, the wind blew the 'For Sale' sign down! Sayes reckons it's an omen. I can't pluck up courage to ask her out. I really am a mardy get.

Went to work at night and cut my thumb wide open, loads of blood everywhere! First aid bloke gave me a brandy, it tasted pot too and then he bandaged me up. I thought I'd get sent home but no chance at this place.

Latics got a good draw away at Alty. I'm missing loads of games 'cos of shift work." (*Drew 1–1 away at Altrincham, NPL. Scorer: Geoff Davies, attendance: 2,865.*)

November 4th, Wednesday... "I hardly slept at all last night, I had a murderous toothache and my thumb was killing me. I lay in until 12 o'clock and then made my lunch.

I went to work and bought a pie on the way for my tea. I also bought some Consulate fags for a change. Work was alright but my teeth were still hurting and so was my thumb but it give over later on.

I went to Paul's on the way home and watched a bit of soccer before running home to see the end. Everton beat Borrussia Moenchengladbach on penalties."

Finally plucked up courage to ask her out. I walked her to the bus stop which took us a long time! She is piggin' great and no danger! I've arranged to go with her again on Sunday."

November 5th, Thursday... "Bonfire night and I had to go to work. I've still got toothache and me thumb is still wreckin' me.

I woke up at noon, had me dinner and went to work. Only me and Kev in today but it was OK 'cos time passed quickly. My thumb opened up again but it looks like it is clotting now. I kept getting blood on the paper samples though.

Dashed back from work to Latics Club only to find that Sayes had been and I missed her, typical! Came home and had a bath, sick."

November 6th, Friday...
"Got up at 8am and called for Paul on the way to Tech. It wasn't bad I suppose but a bit boring. We went into town and I bought Led Zep 111. Paul bought some trousers and we went back to Paul's to listen to my new record, excellent it is too. Paul has hurt his foot so we spent some time at Wigan Infirmary but apparently his foot is OK.

Paul wouldn't come to FAG at night so I went by myself. I talked with Sayes all night and finally plucked up courage to ask her out. I walked her to the bus stop which took us a long time! She is piggin' great and no danger! I've arranged to go with her again on Sunday."

November 7th, Saturday... "Me and Paul had our dinner in the Market, yet another one of Colin Cooke's cheese and onion butties washed down by half a Tartan. 8d for a half is alreet I reckon.

We went to Latics and played soccer in the car park before going to Skem. Not a bad game but we should have won it. We'll ave em at home!" *(1–1 vs Skelmersdale Utd away. FA Cup fourth qualifying round. Scorer: Bobby Todd. Attendance: 5,200.)*

"Got home, had me tea and went to Tech dance with Paul. Great it was too, Paul went with some girl but I came out at 11.15pm and came home."

November 8th, Sunday... "Well it started off so well.

I only got up at 12.45pm to have my dinner. I went to Paul's and we watched soccer on TV. I left to come home to have a bath and a shave, all ready for my night out with Sayes."

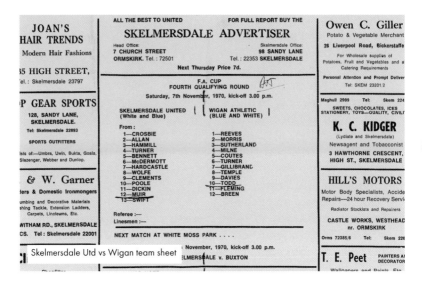

Skelmersdale Utd vs Wigan team sheet

> "I went to Paul's and we walked into town to meet our wenches. Sayes and I decided to go to our house. We met Paul on the way, his wench never showed up!
>
> Me and Sayes had a great time in our house and I walked her into town to get her bus back to Worsley Mesnes. Then at the last moment she tells me she doesn't want to see me proper!"

There were a considerable number of shop doorways on that walk to the bus stop in town. So many that we nearly missed the last bus. I was keen to get on the bus with Sue. I'd have happily walked/floated back home all the way from her house in Worsley Mesnes. But, in a sign of things to come, Sue made a 'sensible' decision. She said she had "enjoyed the night but didn't want to get serious, oh and by the way, get off the bloody bus!" A clip around the ear from the conductor also helped to prise me from her company thus allowing the increasingly angry passengers to get on their way.

> **November 9th, Monday...** "I only got up at 11.30am and I wasn't very happy due to last night's carry on. That finally settles it, the final nail in the coffin and all that, wenches are bloody crackers! Sayes won't start courting again till she is older. She says she has too much schoolwork to do if she wants to be a doctor and all that

stuff. I told her I'll happily be her patient to practise on. It was a real sickener that, so I wrote some poems to prove it.

Paul came round to sympathize. Mum and Dad went out, so we played music until my parents came home and I set off for work feeling shitty. Night shifts again, I hate them."

November 10th, Tuesday... "I got in from work rather shattered. Kev isn't in all week so it's bad all told. I've a good mind to send Sayes a letter but I think I'd rather tell her how I feel to her face.

Paul was going to come round to play records and all that but he phoned to say he wasn't coming so I just watched TV before going out to work. With Kev not in there's only two of us in and it's pretty rough too.

I'm dying to see Sayes again soon!"

November 11th, Wednesday... "Went to bed still feeling a bit sick about Sayes, but it'll soon wear off. Apparently it poured down all day but I slept through it, even with a toothache.

Peaky came round at 6.30pm and we went to meet Paul, Keith and Evvy then we all set off for Latics. It was a great night, reet noisy Kop and we won 5–0. Second half we played really well. *(FA Cup fourth qualifying round replay, vs Skelmersdale Utd. Scorers: Geoff Davies x 2, Derek Temple x 2, and an own goal. Attendance: 5,013.)*

Keith and I walked into town where me and my raging toothache got the bus to work together."

As often proved to be the case, football was the perfect antidote to those teenage lovesick blues. For the next couple of weeks my broken heart was mollified by my love for Wigan Athletic. The development of such coping mechanisms in times of disappointment was to stand me in good stead in years to come. I wish I could say that when the reverse was the case, i.e. on the numerous occasions when Latics broke my heart, girls would provide an equally enjoyable distraction, but this rarely proved to be the case.

Women just didn't get football, "It's only a game for God's sake," would be a defining statement signalling the beginning of the end of many of my relationships with the fairer sex.

November 12th, Thursday... "I had to work with Brian today 'cos Kev is still off and Steve is at Tech. My toothache soon went after a couple of aspirins, Mum reckons it's just wisdom teeth pushing through. I'd rather be thick, I think!

We cribbed most of the tests today and left a load of work for the morning shift, but he's the boss. He left at 6am leaving me on my own for an hour, and I was rushed too.

Got home and read about Latics in the papers then went to bed. I got up, went for a Post, had my tea, had a bath and then went for Paul, who wasn't in. So I went back to work for my wages. It's a long way to go and a nuisance, but it's worth it just to get that brown envelope!"

November 13th, Friday... "I went for Paul at 8.30am and we went to Tech. I just mucked about with Keith all day. Me and Paul went in to town where Paul bought a Black Sabbath LP. We also bought our tickets for the Tech dance tomorrow and then went wom.

We went to FAG at night but it wasn't much good. I went to work at 10 o'clock, not a bad shift really. My new transistor radio arrived today, it is quite LOUD really!"

This was the month that John Toshack signed for Liverpool from Cardiff City for the considerable sum at the time of £110,000. Meanwhile Latics signed Graham Oates from Blackpool for a reported £2,000. I know which of these two signings brought me greater joy over the next few seasons.

November 14th, Saturday... "FAG wur pot last night, crap band and someone reading bloody poetry! Dead boring. I got in from work, had my breakfast and then went to bed. I forced myself to get up at 1pm and had my dinner.

I met Paul at the bottom of Queensway and we went to Latics. We didn't play well but Geoff Davies got yet another hat-trick, his fifth of the season!" *(3–3, vs Kirkby Town, NPL. Att: 3,386.)*

Elsewhere in football, a bizarre incident occurred on this day in 1970 that was to further enhance Bobby Moore's standing in football as one of the 'good guys'. He accidentally hammered a defensive clearance against the referee knocking him out! Moore promptly bent over, retrieved the whistle and blew it to stop the game. What a hero!

"Went to Tech dance at night, not bad but I didn't go with anyone, Paul went with the same wench as last week, I don't even know her name. I walked home with Peaky. I wish I could go out with Sayes again, just once more, that's all."

November 15th, Sunday... "I couldn't be bothered to get up until 1 o'clock again 'cos it was so cold and then there was nothing to do. I had my dinner and that was all. I watched a bit of soccer on TV then went for a walk around town and in the park. Nowt doing so I came home.

A bizarre incident occurred on this day in 1970 that was to further enhance Bobby Moore's standing in football as one of the 'good guys'

At night I went for Paul and persuaded him to come for a drink, he was reluctant because he's got an English exam tomorrow at Tech."

November 16th, Monday... "My new alarm radio woke me up at 5.45am and woke Dad up too! Well, he had to drive to Tyneside anyway so why all the fuss? I made my breakfast and went to work in the pouring rain, I got soaked. Kev actually came in today for a change! It was a fairly easy shift actually. The morning shifts are the best 'cos the work passes quickly, just getting up so early that's the problem.

2 o'clock came soon enough and I got my bus in to Wigan and went to Tech and met Keith. We all booked for the South Shields FA Cup game. At night I went and picked up the tickets, came home and had a bath."

November 17th, Tuesday... "Up nice (?) and early again. The radio woke up the entire house again, I'm not popular.

Work was rotten 'cos there was only me and Steve in and I have to do a load of work taking 'release notes', testing, etc. The morning went slowly but surely. I did a 'Gurley' change and at 2pm I went home."

A 'Gurley' change is not a phonetic spelling error on my part relating to gender re-assignment. Precisely what it indicated in terms of the paper production process I never really understood but it involved measuring the air resistance of paper and it was important.

"It poured down all afternoon and I got soaked going home. Paul and I went to a party at the Tech Club but I went home for an early night."

November 18th, Wednesday... "I'm writing this tomorrow 'cos I didn't yesterday so I'll have to write today's today as well as yesterday's, understood?

I got up at 5.45am again and went to work. It's a good job I've only a day left to pay day 'cos I've got no money left! Work wasn't bad really, it went quick enough 'cos all of us were on shift.

We all went to Gidlow Boys' Speech Day at night, not bad for a laugh I suppose. I got my prize for English, a book about World War Two Prisoners of War under the Japs. We all went for a drink after and I went home tired."

November 19th, Thursday... "Well I'm writing this today, not yesterday or tomorrow, so we're right now aren't we? Are we?

There was only me and Kev in at work and he was moaning like mad all shift because we were quite busy. Still the shift soon passed.

I came home and had a bath after tea. Then I went for Bes and we went to Latics Club where we had five pints too many! It was good to get me sleepy I suppose."

November 20th, Friday... "Well today is my 17th birthday. I got a shirt, some gloves, pyjamas, chocolate, money, and cards.

Went to Tech but I never went in to any classes. Well it's my birthday; they can't really expect me to go in today can they? I don't care; I have to move up to Geordie land soon anyway. I had my tea and bought a bottle of whisky what me and Paul supped and had a laugh at night."

This was probably the first time that I realised birthdays are essentially for kids. In typical teenage fashion I wanted to be treated as an adult except when it suited me, like my birthday. *Then* I wanted to have presents galore, loads of cash gifts and my favourite meal off my mum for tea, beans on toast with a poached egg on top.

> **Didn't want to miss this one! South Shields away in the FA Cup. There was a football special train laid on**

Fancy getting pyjamas for your 17th birthday? I kept this quiet when friends asked what I got for my birthday. The shirt was bright orange, bri-nylon and came in a box, the first shirt I ever had that arrived packaged. I wore it once only and suffered such ridicule that I was delighted when my mum absent-mindedly put her iron through it.

November 21st, Saturday... "I overslept! Mark and Clive, my baby brothers, were sent up to wake me up just as Paul phoned to see where I was. Didn't want to miss this one! South Shields away in the FA Cup. There was a football special train laid on with hundreds of us Latics fans crammed into 15 carriages.

Me, Paul, and loads of us daft lads were all in one coach. We had a riot all day. We supped more ale that I've supped in my entire life and no jesting. I lost my voice before the game started. Bastard railway police kept us waiting on the Tyne Bridge for ages so we just threw loads of bog rolls into the river. The game wasn't so good but we got a draw so it was all right I suppose." *(South Shields away, FA Cup first round proper 1–1. Scorer: Derek Temple. Attendance: 4,500.)*

"I don't know how none of us were arrested today. Every shop we went in got lifted and every railway station we went through on the way back got pelted with bottles of piss, cans, bog rolls and soggy butties.

My dad's new office is in South Shields, he's welcome to it from what I could see. The whole town looks a right dump, and I thought Wigan was bad! I felt rotten when we eventually got in to Wigan so I just went home."

In a strange quirk of fate there were photographs in the Wigan Observer at the time of a Latics competition winner playing football with the players on the sands of Whitley Bay. A young Andrew Roberts, from

Hindley, had won a competition to travel with Latics to the South Shields FA Cup game. This was the very same beach on which I was to spend many happy hours in the ensuing years, though little did I know that at the time.

November 22nd, Sunday... "I slept in until dinner-time, not really surprising after yesterday's performance I suppose is it?

I read the Sunday papers; Latics got quite a mention. I tried to shake off the after-effects of yesterday but I still felt rotten when I went to work. It wore off gradually and I woke up later on.

It was busy at work too. I was very tired by the time 10 o'clock came and glad to get home to my bed."

November 23rd, Monday... "I had a lovely, lazy morning for a change and got up at noon. I read the papers, comics, etc and had my dinner.

I met Paul at Tech and we went into town where I bought a pair of Levi cords Wigan. They're not bad but should look better after a wash or six. I've skived off work, but for a good reason... Latics!!

A load of us daft lads all went to Latics. Great it was too. We had a crowd of 10,592 on and loads of us singing. Great Kop, fantastic atmosphere with a good, solid performance on the pitch. At one point we lost Peaky and Jimmy, never found them either. We won 2–0 and that was all I was bothered about!" *(vs South Shields, FA Cup first round replay. Scorers: Bobby Todd and Derek Temple.)*

November 24th, Tuesday... "I slept in again, very late, about 11am well actually not as late as usual but not bad.

I got up to read about Latics, 10,500 on, great stuff eh? I had my dinner and made my tea before going to work. I expected them to say something about not coming in last night but they didn't! Work was rather boring 'cos there was only two of us on.

Called on Paul on my way home and he had got me a paper, loads about Latics for a change. We've drawn Peterborough at home in the next round, we'll have 'em! All ticket, 25,000 expected, superb, can't wait."

November 25th, Wednesday... "There's only one good thing about this shift and that is that you can lie in all morning, which I did of course.

Kev was actually at work today, the first time since last Thursday. He left at 6 o'clock but not before breaking the balance mucking about with me. We both got suspended for a day for that!

The shift dragged after that but we listened to England on the radio and when I got home I watched the highlights on telly. England beat East Germany 3–1."

November 26th, Thursday... "A telephone call woke me up but I went back to bed and crawled out again about noon. I read the papers, had my dinner, and went out to work. Brian was on with me until about 5.30pm when he went home having cribbed most of the tests! I was by myself until 6.15pm when Steve came in and for once I was pleased to see him.

I called in to the Bier Keller on my home and met Sayes, Judith and Janet. We talked a bit then I walked up Mesnes Road with Janet. From what she said I'll have to think about Sayes again I think?"

> I seem to recall that our host that day was Dave Lee Travis. I'm unsure because I only had eyes for Sayes throughout the entire afternoon

November 27th, Friday... "Mum woke me up at 8am. I haven't told her I've been suspended from Tech, sorry Mum if you're reading this but it is so boring and pointless if we're moving house isn't it? Had my breakfast and went for Paul. I just mucked about Tech all day, doing nothing really, but then I never do anyway!

At dinner-time I went to the 'Radio One Club' at the Casino, and met Sayes. We talked all afternoon and do you know what? I think she is still interested."

The 'Radio One Club' involved national DJs hosting the lunch-time Radio One slot from a series of locations around the country and on this occasion it happened to be Wigan Casino. I seem to recall that our host that day was Dave Lee Travis. I'm unsure because I only had eyes for Sayes throughout the entire afternoon, and indeed for a couple of years thereafter.

"At night I went to FAG and talked to Sayes again. We just click, why won't she start courting proper? Later I went to the Blues Club which was great.

Coming home, me, Peaky and Paul got caught short and had to piss in Makinson's Arcade. A copper come after us and took all our names. We all laughed it off, the copper never laughed. I am afraid and embarrassed now, what if we get done just for that?"

November 28th, Saturday... "I got up at 10.30am full of dread, wondering if the coppers would come. I went in town with Paul and did nothing but worry really.

Latics played pot so that didn't help at all and only equalised with an own goal." *(vs Scarborough at home, NPL. Drew 1–1. Scorer: Dunne. Att: 4,026.)* "We have discovered that the copper who charged us is the brother of a pal of ours, Wink, so we've asked him, with some force, to persuade his brother to think again."

> **Coming home, me, Peaky and Paul got caught short and had to piss in Makinson's Arcade. A copper come after us and took all our names**

I was mortified at the thought of the police calling round and charging me with 'urinating in a public place'. The sheer humiliation of it all! If I'd been done for street fighting, under age drinking or even football hooliganism, well fair enough. At least there'd be some street cred involved earning respect from my peers. But pissing in a shop doorway? Do me a favour! To my mind at the time, it was all Wigan council's fault for closing the public toilets at 10 o'clock at night, just when folk needed a toilet the most.

"Went to Tech Club at night; Rag-Week Dance. It wasn't bad. I went with Sayes again and Paul with another wench. I walked Sayes to her bus stop, she really is special. Then I walked back home with Peaky and Jimmy. Dave Wink's brother has let us off, thank God!"

November 29th, Sunday... "I had a lovely lie-in without having to worry about any coppers coming. What a marvellous feeling it was too and no danger! I read the papers and had my dinner before going round to Paul's where we watched soccer on TV. Peaky came round and we just talked and listened to the radio until tea-time.

Peaky came for me later and we went to the Bier Keller for a drink. On the way home we called in to Chris's. When I got in I read a belting newspaper article about Latics."

November 30th, Monday... "I couldn't sleep last night at all and it was probably about 4am before I got to sleep. I made up for it by sleeping in until 1pm!

After dinner I went into town to pay the electric bill for Mum. I met up with Keith, Evvy and Paul and we all walked up for a paper.

I phoned Janet and asked her to ask Sayes to phone me. A load of us all went to Latics at night. We played pot but won 4–0. Pot game, poor crowd, went to work, bloody night shifts again." *(vs Lancaster City, Lancashire Floodlit Cup. Scorers: Temple, Todd, Morris and Savage. Att: 1,268.)*

AN INTERVIEW WITH
GEOFF DAVIES

A New Hero Is Born

I had long mourned the loss of my 'hero', Tony McLoughlin. But such is the fickle nature of football fans everywhere, particularly young fans, it wasn't long before a new object of my devotion emerged.

Geoff Davies had signed for Wigan during the summer. He proved to be a snip at £800 although I've no doubt Northwich Victoria saw it as a good piece of business given the transfer fees of the times. He started the 1970-71 season on fire, rattling in goals and hat-tricks with complete freedom. I had vague memories of Geoff playing for Northwich the previous season but I certainly hadn't expected him to make the kind of impact he did. Tall, gangly and athletic, Geoff Davies thrived on the service provided by a vibrant Latics side that created chances from all over the pitch.

Geoff Davies

A few years ago my fellow Latics fan, Tony Topping, caught up with Geoff many years after the events described in this diary. The full interview is included here.

Geoff, what were your early days like as a fledgling footballer and whom did you support as a child?

"I played football at school, which was 20 miles away from home, and was selected to play for Wirral Schoolboys. Shrewsbury Town showed an interest in me but my dad wanted me to have a trade so when I left school I started a five-year apprenticeship with Shell as a vehicle fitter. I then signed part time for my home town club Ellesmere Port Town in the Cheshire League who were managed by the ex-Everton player Jimmy Harris. I started out as a winger but because of the amount of goals I was scoring Jimmy switched me to centre forward. I was watched by Shrewsbury Town, Port Vale, Chester, Wrexham and Tranmere but nothing materialized.

The following season the club nearly folded and they started to sell their better players. Northwich Victoria then approached me so I accepted a move to the Drill Field side.

As a child aged 6–10 years old I travelled regularly by coach to watch the great Wolves side managed by Stan Cullis with players like Billy Wright, etc, great players and great games. When I stopped travelling I became a Liverpool supporter and I still am to this day."

Wigan Athletic were one of the biggest non-league clubs in the country in 1970, how did you feel that when you joined them? You scored 5 hat-tricks in your first three months so the move obviously worked for you.

"After a couple of weeks I knew we were going to be successful. I watched and learned from players like Gordon Milne and Jim Fleming, they had a great work ethic. Gordon was a great leader and motivator and he led by example. My all round game improved and with it belief and self-esteem. I was surrounded by good players and good people. For me as a striker who was constantly making runs into goal scoring positions, it was a delight to be supported by the wing play of Derek Temple and Graham Oates; their service was superb. They had the Beckham-like ability to pick me out. I also had through balls provided from midfield by Gordon Milne and Jim Fleming. Was it any wonder I scored 42 goals that season?

We had the hard working Bobby Todd closing down the midfield and a terrifically strong defence led by Ian Gillibrand."

Of all the stars of that 70/71 team who was your closest pal and who did you most admire as a player?

"I admired everyone on the team, the backroom boys and especially the fantastic Wigan supporters and people. My closest friends were Dennis Reeves, Kenny Morris, Lee Koo and Bobby Todd.

I travelled up the M6 three or four times a week with Dennis Reeves in all kinds of foul winter weather, fog, rain, gales and snow. Everyone on the team was close there were no cliques. Trips away were great, especially Majorca, well apart from having to listen to Derek Temple's Bee Gees records all the time!"

What's your greatest memory from your time at Wigan?

"The FA Cup runs were great and we deserved all the victories. The Wigan supporters came out in their thousands and carried us along. We played in some terrible conditions, snow and heavy mud but we always kept our shape combined with our attacking style and a tremendous work rate.

I will always remember the Manchester City cup game and the build up to it. Today it would be like playing Manchester United because of the great players City had in their team at that time. There was a full house at Maine Road and we were on Match of the Day. I would love a copy of that game.

We played well and deserved a replay, the game hinged on two moments, Dennis Reeves boot split and he mishit his goal kick which resulted in the only goal, and Joe Corrigan's wonder save on to the post from my header in the last minute. I have photographs of that moment and I often think of what might have been if that had gone in."

You scored 22 goals the following season and then left to join Chester City. Did you enjoy your experience there?

"When I joined, Derek Draper was first choice centre forward and I was told he was retiring but this never happened, and with Derek being a big favourite with the management and fans, I struggled to gain a regular first team place. I lost my confidence but I scored regularly for the reserves, once scoring six against Port Vale. Gordon Lee, the Vale manager, was interested in signing me but so too were other clubs and I signed for Wrexham manager John Neal."

Your league career really took off at Wrexham.

"It was one of the best moves I ever made. John Neal was a wonderful manager. We reached the quarter-finals of the FA Cup in 73/74 before losing to a deflected goal at Burnley. We had played well in earlier rounds but didn't perform on the

day. It was the first time that I witnessed players crying in the changing room. We won the Welsh Cup the following season and I enjoyed playing in the European Cup Winners' Cup."

After your success with Wrexham you went to play in America. What was that like?

"I had already spent a summer there when I was at Wrexham playing for Boston Minutemen. In my first game I lined up with former Portuguese players Eusebio, Calardo, and Fernando Nelson. Uruguayan international Soroa and West Germans Neumann and Suhnholtz were also in the side and I finished up top scorer.

In my second spell I returned to Boston and my first game was against New York Cosmos who had Pele in their side. I then got transferred to Chicago Sting managed by former Man Utd player Bill Foulkes. While I was there Bill told me that when I was at Wigan, Manchester United had put in a bid for me but it was turned down, I never knew about the offer.

In 1976 I returned to England to sign for Port Vale, a move that didn't work out and included being loaned out to Hartlepool. I returned to America playing for San Jose Earthquakes along with Trevor Hockey and Alan Birchenall. Other league players included George Best, Beckenbauer, Cruyff, Chingalia, Rodney Marsh and many others."

You then returned to England for one last league season with Wimbledon.

"Dave Bassett recommended me to them and Alan Batsford the manager and chairman Ron Noades came to my house in Chester to sign me. Ron was in his Rolls Royce! I played in their first ever league game a 3–3 draw with Halifax. At this time I played as a defensive midfielder and was enjoying my time until Dario Gradi took over as manager. He made it clear he didn't want any older players in his side. I just never got on with Gradi.

I went back to the States to play for Los Angeles Skyhawks and San Francisco Fog. I then began to coach at soccer camps *and even trained to be a hairdresser and met Vidal Sassoon! After brief spells with Northwich and Caernarfon Town, I returned to America for good. My last team was Los Angeles where I was lucky enough to become head coach. I now live in San Francisco where I am a fully licensed coach training some of the best youth players in California at team and summer camps."*

This interview took place over a matter of months with many emails flying back and forth across the Atlantic. In all that time Geoff has been courteous and friendly in the extreme, no task has been too much. He is a warm and generous man who richly deserves his place in the Wigan Athletic Hall of Fame.

DECEMBER 1970

And so to the final diary entry of what has been a momentous year for our young diarist and, indeed, for Wigan Athletic F.C.

From a bolshy, moody schoolboy, to a frustrated, unsettled laboratory apprentice. From Ian McNeill, Tony Mac and Kharkov, to 'Sir' Gordon Milne, Derek Temple and Peterborough Utd. (With Man City in the FA Cup, just two days after the diary ends). A myopic, parochial view of life continues with little impact from, or upon, the outside world. Our diarist continues his introspective, self-centred view of Wigan and his world of 1970.

December 1st, Tuesday... "I'll have to think of something to write 'cos I spent all day in bed, lovely! I got up in time for tea and then Janet phoned to say that Sayes had not been to school. So I wrote her a letter instead of the chat I intended, and why not indeed?

I went for Paul and we went for a couple of pints in the Students' Union Club (SU). Then I missed my bus for work, crawling in an hour and a half late!"

> Turns out Dad has bought a house in a place called Whitley Bay, (boo!). Wonder if they have a decent football team? Do I really have to go?

December 2nd Wednesday... "29 days to go to the end of this diary, I'm sure it will be interesting to read in a few years time!

Got in from work and went to bed very tired as usual. I got up praying and hoping Sayes would phone and she did! It really lifted me just talking to her. Brent Gore is having a party on Saturday and Sayes has agreed to come with me so I could be in there?

Paul, Curly and I had a couple of pints before I went off to work where there was only me and Kev in again, there's supposed to be three on each shift.

Turns out Dad has bought a house in a place called Whitley Bay, (boo!). Wonder if they have a decent football team? Do I really have to go?"

It transpired that Whitley Bay did indeed possess a very good football team at the time and I was delighted to be able to retain my non-league football roots. Over the years I became an avid fan. I'm pleased to say I witnessed probably their finest hour when Whitley Bay FC knocked Preston North End out of the FA Cup in 1989 beating them 2–0, much to the joy of my fellow Latics fans. I like to think it was my Wigan presence that tipped the scales against the 'nob-enders' as we politely called them. Whitley Bay FC provided a ready replacement for my enthusiasm for non-league football easing the pain of leaving Wigan. In May 2009 I joined 7,000 Whitley Bay FC fans on the journey to the new Wembley where another 'North End' were again beaten 2-0. This time it was the mighty Glossop North End put to the sword on an occasion reminiscent to me of Latics 1973 FA Trophy Final at the old Wembley. Thus, my love affair with non-league football continues to this day.

> Barclay James Harvest, Slade and, I recall through a drunken haze, Joe Cocker, (though it could have been an impersonator for all I know!), all appeared as relative unknowns

December 3rd, Thursday... "Cos there was only Kevin and me on last night, I was knackered when I got in so I went straight to bed and sleeeeeep! I got up at 6 o'clock and had a bath, washed my hair and went in to work to collect my wages.

Paul was with his wench at night so I just went home and watched Tom Jones on TV before going to bed. I couldn't sleep at all; I've only been up six hours!"

December 4th, Friday... "I went to Tech but I didn't go in classes 'cos I was behind before we started. I mucked about with Brent and Keith then went with Brent and bought Jimi Hendrix. 'Band of Gypsys.' Great it is too.

I went to FAG but there was no-one in so I went to SU Club. Met Sayes who changed her mind and said she wouldn't come to the party. But I managed to persuade her, thank God. Big row it was. As a result I missed my bus and was late for work, I only got in at 10-past 11 but nobody said owt."

The Students' Union club was a ramshackle but magical place. Demolished approx 1972, the club was situated behind what is now Swinley Labour Club on Wigan Lane (across from the Bowling Green). Run down to the point of nigh dereliction it became home from home.

Just getting to the door involved a treacherous slide through mud and shale. Sunderland fans, with their affection for mud-sliding would have loved it. The gents' toilets were outside and thank God they were too, the smell would have made a pig weep. But beer was cheap, Newcastle Brown freely available with no questions asked regarding age, and most important of all, the music was superb.

Barclay James Harvest, Slade and, I recall through a drunken haze, Joe Cocker, (though it could have been an impersonator for all I know!), all appeared as relative unknowns. The rock and blues music was loud, raw and took no prisoners. Love it or hate it, to me and my pals it was the only place to go. The Tufty Club was off the social radar for evermore.

December 5th, Saturday... "Got in from night shift and made Mum and Dad a cup of tea and toast. Read the papers and Sayes's letter. She is too nice to get nasty with! Went to bed dreaming of Sayes and tonight!

I got up at 2.30pm when Brent phoned telling me to go to his house. We sorted out all the beer for the party tonight and I came home. Lay on my bed waiting for Latics result on the radio, we won 2–1, great." *(vs South Shields away, NPL. Scorers: Geoff Davies and Graham Oates. Att: 1,013.)*

"Sayes was dead late, kept me waiting at the bottom of Makinson's Arcade for ages. The strap had broken on her shoes but we went to Brent's party. It was great, loads of ale and wow-wee, me and Sayes got really close!

We managed to miss her bus home so I plucked up courage and asked my dad if he could give Sayes a lift home. Luckily he'd been for a drink with Danny so he was in a good mood though he did use the back roads to avoid the police."

December 6th, Sunday... "Oh it was great last night. I really felt close to Sayes for once.

This flu outbreak was the back-end of the infamous 'Hong Kong' variant and was particularly unpleasant. Between 1969 and 1970 it was estimated that there were some 30,000 fatalities in the UK

I got up at 11.30am and went to the Royal Oak and met Robby, Eric and them. We went to Marsh Green to play football but the pitch was waterlogged so they called the game off. Pot that were, I really wanted to play."

> "Paul, Brent, Chris, Peaky and the rest of us all went
> SU Cub at night. We drank and talked, then went to
> Brent's and drank and talked some more!
> If only Sayes would go out with me proper?"

At this point in my life and with no warning whatsoever, disaster struck!

Just as things were coming together nicely with my girlfriend, and with the Latics-Peterborough FA Cup match just days away, I succumbed to a nasty dose of influenza. This flu outbreak was the back-end of the infamous 'Hong Kong' variant and was particularly unpleasant. Between 1969 and 1970 it was estimated that there were some 30,000 fatalities in the UK alone. This may not have been Swine Flu but it certainly made me pig sick at the time.

There were no early warning signs or symptoms to suggest that flu was on its way. I felt fine one day, wretched the next. It is often said that one way of establishing the difference between a heavy cold and flu is the following.

If you get out of bed and notice a £20 note lying in the garden, with a cold you'd go down and retrieve it, with flu, you'd just say "sod it" and clamber back into bed!

In my case it was different however. Having not missed a single game, home or away in Latics' FA Cup run, I was desperate to attend the Peterborough game. With a huge crowd expected, a potential shock on the cards, and all the publicity this would generate, this game was all that mattered as I lay in my sick-bed.

With a heavy cold I would have gone to the game regardless, but the flu? It was just not possible. When my parents enforced the doctor's advice and forbade me going anywhere near Springfield Park (or any

E PARTIES	—	FOOTBALL EXCURSIONS	—	HOLIDAYS IN BRITAIN AND

TERN
· all

RES

ΛIRS
ΞRVICE

N

WIGAN ATHLETIC
Royal Blue Shirts
White Shorts

1. D. REEVES
2. A. TURNER
3. W. SUTHERLAND
4. G. MILNE
5. D. COUTTS
6. I. GILLIBRAND
From—
7. J. SAVAGE
8. R. TODD
9. G. DAVIES
10. J. FLEMING

Aπ 17,300

PETERBOROUGH UNITED

1. M. DREWERY
2. F. NOBLE
3. J. DUNCLIFFE
4. J. ILEY
5. J. WILE
6. B. WRIGHT
7. R. MOSS
8. C. GARWOOD
9. J. HALL
10. P. PRICE
11. T. ROBSON

Substitute

HARRY Ν
LTD
HALLGATE,
Telephone
Wallpapers & \

Crown
Sanderson
Shand Kyᴄ
I.C.I.
Walflair
Lincrusta-\
Anaglypta
Vymura and C

Wigan vs Peterborough Utd team sheet

HARD WORKING WIGAN ATHLETIC STRIKER GEOFF DAVIES CAUSES CONCERN IN THE PETERBOROUGH DEFENCE AS HE MOVES IN ON A HIGH CENTRE.

where else for that matter) it was with some real, if well disguised, relief. That game was my £20 note test.

Nine days entries in the diary simply read "ILL", and even these were entered retrospectively. So for those of you who ring in sick at work claiming to have flu, just think again!

It was a well-timed illness however as I slept through a series of power cuts brought about by a 'work to rule' by power workers. This in turn saw shops in Wigan sell out of candles as the UK experienced the run-up to what was dubbed 'the Candle Light Christmas.'

For the record, despite having played six games in fourteen days, Wigan Athletic beat Peterborough United 2–1. Scorers were Geoff Davies and Jim Fleming with a last minute penalty. The attendance was 17,300 (minus one), the biggest of the entire FA Cup round by a long way.

"What Price Wigan Athletic for the League Now?" asked the 'Wigan Observer'.

December 16th, Wednesday... "I felt a lot better today, at last but still only got up at 12 o'clock. Generous as ever, I appear to have given my flu to our Mark.

I stayed in until 4 o'clock then went for a paper and called in on Paul but he wur out. Latics have drawn Man City away in the next round! Fantastic!!!"

"Later on me and Paul went to the SU Club for a drink, it was good to be out but the ale tasted funny. Me, Paul, and a bunch of mates all went to a woman's house on Wigan Lane, she wur called Pat *(I think)*. She wur a teacher at Tech but I'd never seen her before. It wur all reet but I still felt rough so I came home."

December 17th, Thursday... "I had another lovely lie-in this morning; I may as well make the best of it while I can! Mark, Clive and Robert have all got the flu now so they are all in bed and my parents are blaming me.

I took a parcel and some Christmas cards to the Post Office on my way to work for my wages. I picked up my wages from the pay office then had to wait forty-five minutes for a bus.

Goofy came to Paul's for a short while, then we went to the SU Club for a drink but I still feel weak so I came home, had a bath and went to bed."

> Got my chips and went off to night shift. Not much Christmas spirit at Cooke & Nuttall's paper mill, but it's a job I suppose

December 18th, Friday... "I slept in again until 12 o'clock! I felt great when I got up apart from being a bit deaf. I read the papers and Robert's comic, well he can't, he's ill in bed and will never know. According to the Wigan Observer, Latics are dead certs for the league now.

I went to the SU Club for a pint but had to leave an hour later to come home and look after the kids 'cos they're still ill.

At night we all went to the SU Club again, it was pot, so we had a drink in town and I was home for midnight."

December 19th, Saturday... "I got up at 10am and went into town. I got knackered doing some Christmas shopping. The flu has took a lot out of me. Now all my brothers have it. Still, I got all the presents I need, I think. I wrapped them all up and watched 'On The Ball'.

Latics was pot. Gordon got a last minute winner but they deserved it I suppose." *(vs Northwich Victoria, NPL. Won 1–0. Scorer: Gordon Milne. Att: 3,375.)*

"Went to Students' Union Club again at night. Spent all night with Sayes then she did her usual vanishing trick so I just sat and got merry before coming home at midnight."

December 20th, Sunday... "Got up late, Brent called round to arrange a game of soccer. Me and Paul met up with them all at Woodfield. Great it was but I wur short of breath and I've got blisters on my feet now as well.

Stewy, Paul and me all went for a pint in the 'Cherry Gardens' then went into Chrissy's to watch a great play on telly."

December 21st, Monday... "Had to get up early to watch the kids again while Mum went shopping. I got a Christmas card off Judith which was a pleasant surprise.

Me and Paul went for our tickets for the Christmas Eve dance at SU Club but there was no-one there so we just talked to Steve and played soccer.

I went for Paul and we got our tickets for Latics. We had a pint then I got my chips and went off to night shift. Not much Christmas spirit at Cooke & Nuttall's paper mill, but it's a job I suppose."

December 22nd Tuesday... "As I think I've said before, there isn't much to write in a diary when you've been in bed all day!

I got up in time for tea but I've got a rotten headache. Watched telly before going round to Paul's. Guess what? He's in bed with flu! So I went in town for a pint before getting some chips and a cup of horrible coffee and set off for work. Work wasn't bad really 'cos there's three of us on all week."

December 23rd, Wednesday... "I was quite tired when I got home but I had my breakfast – sausage and eggs on toast. Read the papers and went to bed.

I woke up with a splitting headache again; both my eyes were killing me. I had a bath but that seemed to make it worse. I went to Paul's and the headache cleared up slowly. I don't think Paul has had proper flu 'cos he's OK now."

"By the time I got to work it was gone, *(my headache and sore eyes, not work!)*. Shift went well."

December 24th, Thursday... "I caught the 6.40am bus from work. I wasn't really tired so had some breakfast and read the papers, maybe I'm excited 'cos it's Christmas?

For a pleasant change I didn't have a headache when I got up. I went for Paul and bought a bottle of whisky. We soon supped that and set off to the SU Club.

It was a riot, I kissed loads of wenches and Sayes a lot but she wouldn't let me walk her home, she is so infuriating. I crawled home at 1 o'clock. I tried not to wake my two little brothers, failed, Mum and Dad not very happy."

December 25th, Friday; Christmas Day... "Well it snowed yesterday, not much but enough to give us the first White Christmas I can remember for years. I got up about 10 o'clock unable to ignore the kids' noise, they are certainly better! I crawled downstairs with a hangover and got my meagre presents. I got a shirt and cuff-links off Mum and £3 quid off Dad but that was basically that.

Paul and I had a few drinks at his house then went up to Stewie's house but there was nowt doing in town, it were pot. I bought a hamburger and came home feeling chep 'cos of Sayes last night. We really like each other but she wants to be free."

Out of interest, the best selling singles at Christmas 1970 were:

1) **'I Hear You Knocking'**   Dave Edmunds.
2) **'Grandad'**   Clive Dunn. (AAAGGGHHH!!!)
3) **'When I'm Dead and Gone'** McGuiness Flint.

What was the best selling album I hear you ask? Well at Christmas, very sadly it was 'Andy Williams Greatest Hits.' Little wonder your scribe was turning to drink at such a tender age.

'Bridge Over Troubled Water' by Simon and Garfunkle spent 24 weeks in the charts in 1970. I remember finding the album miserable at the time.

December 26th, Saturday... "Boxing Day... and I slept in until 1pm. We only had soup and cheese butties for dinner 'cos we all got up so late."

"I went for Paul, and we stopped in his house playing music, smoking and supping while we waited for the football results to come up. Latics won! Happy Christmas!!" *(2–1 away at Northwich Victoria, NPL. Scorers: Pope own goal and ? Att: 2,275. It cost 8s at Eavesways for the coach trip which is why I didn't go.)*

"It has managed to snow on Christmas Eve, Christmas Day and now Boxing Day! Not deep though.

We went to SU Club again at night and Sayes dun it again. She stayed with me all night; drinking, talking, hugging and kissing and then, right at the end... piddl't off with her pals. She wouldn't let me walk her home or owt. So I came home and watched Man Utd 4–4 Derby on TV then wrote Sayes a strongly worded letter."

> Bridge Over Troubled Water' by Simon and Garfunkle spent 24 weeks in the charts in 1970. I remember finding the album miserable at the time

If there seems to be a lot of letter writing going in these pages readers should remember that there were no mobile phones, no texts or emails. Using a land line meant having to speak to a family member, maybe even, horror of horrors, the girl's dad! (Or even worse, a smart-arsed little brother.)

On the broader front, if our young diarist had extricated his head from his backside for a few moments he may have been saddened by the death of Lillian Board, the Golden Girl of UK athletics. She died of bowel cancer in Munich. Strange how Christmas always brings tragedy?

At a local level, December 1970 saw the Wigan Observer report vandals desecrating gravestones in Beech Hill, and we think ill of the kids of today?

December 27th, Sunday... "Just three days to the end of this diary! I had a lovely lie-in until three o'clock when Mum woke me up, and I had my dinner.

I went up to Woodfield and played football until it snowed too hard to carry on.

Stew came after 'Please Sir' and a bunch of us all

went to SU Club. It was good for a laugh. We all got very drunk then went to Chrissy's after and got even more drunk."

December 28th, Monday... "I hardly slept a wink last night, too piss't. I got up at 5.45am very thirsty. Got to work at 7am but Kev came in late and Steve not at all. It went pretty quickly but then this shift usually does.

The bus into Wigan was late then broke down but I legged it and got to Latics at 3.05pm just in time for a great game. Fantastic performance all round, we wuz top of the league and them second but we 'ammered 'em 4–1." *(vs Stafford Rangers, NPL. Scorers: Milne, Fleming (pen), Oates and Davies. Att: 8,137.)*

"Great atmosphere, loads of singing and that, all ready for Man City in five days time. Play like that and we have a chance? At night me and Paul went to SU Club, not bad, somewhere to go I suppose."

December 29th, Tuesday... "Got up at 6am and scoffed a breakfast. I caught an earlier bus than usual and got to work early. Dave Challander was on with us 'cos he'd swapped a shift with Steven. It went all right really.

Loads about Latics in the paper and they were even on TV on the local 6 o'clock news. I met Paul and bought a pair of shoes in town and my ticket for the Man City game. At night me and Paul had a drink in the club."

December 30th, Wednesday... "I had to get up at 6am again today, ridiculous time. Work went dead quick though and we had finished by 12.30pm so we all went to the Crown in Horwich for Cooke & Nuttall's Xmas drink. It was a good laugh actually though the journey home wasn't."

This was the occasion when another lesson in life was driven home to me with some force.

Never, ever, under any circumstances, should you drink numerous pints of beer and then, with a 16 year-old, inexperienced bladder, get on a shuddering, slow moving bus. What started as a feeling of slight discomfort rapidly developed into mild panic followed by excruciating agony as I fought the urge to unleash a deluge, of Niagara Falls dimensions, down the steps of the bus.

The bus driver seemed to stop at every possible bus stop even when there was no-one waiting or alighting. Some of these he had never stopped at before, and of course he drove as slowly as possible. Every set of traffic lights were on red, every roundabout snarled up. I felt each bump and tight corner. This was clearly a deliberate act on the part of this vindictive, sadistic bus driver.

> Never, ever, under any circumstances, should you drink numerous pints of beer and then, with a 16 year-old, inexperienced bladder, get on a shuddering, slow moving bus

I was becoming delirious. It got to the point where the only thing that mattered in life was relieving my swollen bladder. Eventually I rushed down the stairs and jumped off the bus, sweeping women and children before me. I found the nearest alleyway and, oblivious to any passers by, let forth a stream of steaming hot piss that seemed to last for ever. The relief was a mixture of pleasure and pain. I went into shock, trembling and weak-kneed. A longer than usual walk home allowed me to indulge my feelings of utter relief and at the same time contempt for the driver.

Latics for the Football League!

N LTD., WIGAN

ON BEHALF OF 305,000 PEOPLE...

The poor chap was, of course, utterly innocent and he knew nothing of my predicament until I leapt off his bus in such dramatic fashion. I have spent the rest of my life ensuring that the 'full bladder – slow bus' equation has never been repeated.

"I bought a paper and came home my tea to find that our Clive has now got the measles!

I went to Paul's for an hour during which time some girl, probably Sayes, called for me but as our Robert answered the door we're none the wiser. He didn't even get a name never mind a message. I stayed in all evening."

We play Man City in 2 days time, I can't wait! Everyone I know is going. I reckon Wigan town centre will be empty on Saturday! Surely they'll let us in the Football League now?

December 31st, Thursday; New Year's Eve... "I had a lovely lie-in today, just for once, until 12 noon. I had to stay in and look after the kids but I had a bath then when my mum came back in I went and got a paper, loads in about Latics for a change. It's because we play Man City in 2 days time, I can't wait! Everyone I know is going. I reckon Wigan town centre will be empty on Saturday! Surely they'll let us in the Football League now?

Well I had a good tea and went round to Brent's. Then I went to SU Club for the New Year's Eve Dance which was good for a laugh. Sayes said she wasn't coming so Paul and I just sat and got very drunk. Paul had his coat nicked which spoiled things but I got in home at 2.30am very piss't."

POSTSCRIPT

So ended a year in the life of one young lad. There were to be no more cold nights scribbling away furtively consigning a life to paper. But what happened to us all I hear you ask? Or not, as the case may be.

Within a few days of the diary ending, Wigan Athletic enjoyed arguably one of their greatest ever days, away at European Cup Winners' Cup holders Manchester City in the FA Cup third round. After dominating long periods of the game and missing a host of chances, a goalkeeping error allowed Colin Bell to score the winner. Despite this display and emerging as NPL Champions by six points at the end of the 1970/71 season, Latics had to wait a further seven painful years to achieve Football League status.

The latest chapter in Latics' existence, the Whelan years, is either the stuff of fairy tales or a commercially based sell-out of the club's very soul depending on your point of view. It has to be said that Latics would most probably be in a sorry state without Dave Whelan. I acknowledge that and in some ways I'm grateful. On the other hand Latics would have survived in one form or another and we, the true fans, would still be supporting them.

Sometimes I have to remind myself that when we play Man Utd or Arsenal we do so on almost equal terms. We are no longer the little minnows taking on the big boys. And yet if I am utterly truthful, I still yearn for those magical days of being the underdogs, of being an up-and-coming club always looking ahead to the next stage of progression. Sometimes it is better to have unfulfilled dreams, the Champions League maybe?

As for myself; within just a few months of the diary ending I had left Wigan. I was dragged, kicking and screaming, to what actually turned out to be an enjoyable new life on Tyneside, this despite the anguish of losing my dad just three years later.

But my love of Latics continued unabated. Having moved to Whitley Bay I spent every decimal 'new pence' I could muster on trips back to Wigan to watch Latics and see my friends. Of course it wasn't the same. People moved on and changed, the town of Wigan changed, even Latics changed. On the visits to where I still called 'home' I felt increasingly like a piece of a jigsaw from the wrong box, I no longer fitted in.

At the same time however I was putting down roots on Tyneside

Still fartin' about; Amsterdam 06

where the locals gradually accepted, and then adopted me, as one of their own. The reputation for friendliness of the 'Geordie Nation' was, and remains, well deserved.

Whilst Latics and I have continued our close relationship to the present day, the same cannot be said of Sue (Sayes) and me. Although we remained close for a few years, constantly writing and phoning each other, it was never going to work out for us. We met up occasionally and it was almost as if we'd never been apart. But we both gradually moved on in our lives, she studied medicine in Leeds whereas I was training to be a nurse in Newcastle upon Tyne.

I last saw Sue in 1977 not long after I'd married; we had just gone our separate ways I suppose. I have never heard from her since, something I profoundly regret.

Paul, as I have mentioned elsewhere in this book, continues to live and thrive in Wigan. He rarely misses a home game being a season-ticket holder. A few years ago Paul suffered the embarrassment of being proclaimed as "Wigan Athletics' Best Ever Supporter" by a national Sunday tabloid newspaper. I'm not sure he has ever forgiven his wife, Anna, for nominating him!

Paul and I stay in regular contact. I see him each time I travel down from Scotland to watch Latics, usually five or six times a season. We have been good friends now for well over forty years. Long may it continue.

> I last saw Sue in 1977 not long after I'd married; we had just gone our separate ways I suppose. I have never heard from her since, something I profoundly regret

I met Judith recently whilst researching this book. She still lives in the Wigan area and looks little different. She seems to have calmed down a bit though and has apparently mastered her irritating fringe!

I was able to track down Bes and spoke to him for the purposes of this book. He continues to live and work in Wigan as an electrician. It was the first time we had spoken for 39 years and thus rather stilted but we did arrange to meet up next time I go 'home' to Wigan. Surely he has calmed down also?

Cooke & Nuttall's paper mill never recovered from my departure. It staggered on until it eventually closed down in 1983 and was subsequently demolished. I understand that one of the mill chimneys remains, preserved as a 'listed building.'

Danny remains, well 'Danny'! He can be opinionated, awkward and cantankerous whilst at the same time loyal, friendly and helpful. Even in his seventies he can still drink me, and most others, under the table. Having once been a 'rugby mon' ("Latics'll never gerr in t'league, Kenneth!") he has in recent years, seen the light, and is now a devoted Latics fan. Danny goes to most games, home and away, so long as he doesn't have to pay.

There are so many others I have mentioned in the diary that I cannot hope to remain informed about. Sadly some of them are no longer with us. Such is the way of life. We all grow up, move on and eventually depart.

I dearly hope I have caused no one offence, it was all a long time ago and we were all so young weren't we?

And so to the people of Wigan in general and Latics fans in particular, I thank you all. On the frequent occasions I return, I find the same friendliness, humour and welcome that I have always felt.

> On the frequent occasions I return, I find the same friendliness, humour and welcome that I have always felt

Of some of my contemporaries however, I do wonder if spending my formative years in Wigan and forging a career in mental health is more than just a coincidence!

Ken Barlow

About The Author

Ken Barlow (who predates the more illustrious TV character by some ten years) is 55 years old. He is married with two grown up daughters and a grandson who is surely destined to become the captain of England (or Scotland) and Wigan Athletic.

An ill fated career in the paper production industry was followed by brief sojourns in the enlightening fields of floor sweeping at Woolworths, and bar-keeping in discos. After an even briefer period in HM Royal Navy Ken found himself on Tyneside in 1972 working in a local psychiatric hospital. This proved to be the beginning of a career stretching for almost forty years in mental health nursing.

Ken has worked in various mental health services in Northern England and Scotland, mainly in community mental health settings and has somehow emerged with a BA and a Masters degree.

Although he still occasionally kicks a ball around an increasingly large 6-a-side football pitch, Ken also enjoys coarse fishing, walking, reading and spending time with his grandson.

As readers may surmise this is Ken's first venture into the non-academic world of publishing.

Yep, 1970 was a long time ago for all of us. The Edgar Broughton Band's current line-up